Five hundred copies of this book, done to commemorate Mike Resnick's Guest of Honorship at Disclave, May 25-28, 1990, the annual convention of the Washington (D.C.) Science Fiction Society (WSFA), were signed and numbered 1-500 by the author; a small additional amount barely sufficient to confound bibliographers were Roman Numbered and signed as presentation copies. This is copy number:

389

Mike Resnick

THROUGH DARKEST RESNICK
WITH GUN AND CAMERA

Science Fiction Books by Mike Resnick

The Goddess of Ganymede
Pursuit on Ganymede
Redbeard
Battlestar Galactica #5:
     Galactica Discovers Earth
The Soul Eater
Birthright: The Book of Man
Walpurgis III
Sideshow
The Three-Legged Hootch Dancer
The Wild Alien Tamer
The Best Rootin' Tootin' Shootin'
     Gunslinger in the Whole Damned Galaxy
The Branch
Eros Ascending
Eros at Zenith
Eros Descending
Eros at Nadir
Adventures
Santiago: A Myth of the Far Future
Stalking the Unicorn: A Fable of Tonight
The Dark Lady: A Romance of the Far Future
Ivory: A Legend of Past and Future
Paradise: A Chronicle of a Distant World
Second Contact
Soothsayer
Oracle
Prophet

Through Darkest

RESNICK

With Gun & Camera

by Mike Resnick

1990
The Press of
The Washington Science Fiction Association, Inc.

"Why Africa?" originally appeared in *Fosfax* #137, copyright © 1989 by Mike Resnick.

"The Lost Race" originally appeared as a chapter in *Adventures*, copyright © 1985 by Mike Resnick.

"Stalking the Perfect Safari" originally appeared in *The Cincinnati Post*, copyright © 1986 by Mike Resnick.

"What I Did On My Winter Vacation" originally appeared in *Lan's Lantern* #20, copyright © 1986 by Mike Resnick

"Stalking the Unicorn With Gun and Camera" originally appeared in the *Magazine of Fantasy and Science Fiction*, copyright © 1986 by The Mercury Press.

"Jumbo" originally appeared in *Swara* (Vol. 9, #6), copyright © 1986 by Mike Resnick.

"The Hunter" originally appeared in slightly different form as a chapter in *Ivory*, copyright © 1988 by Mike Resnick.

"What I Did on My Summer Vacation" originally appeared in *Lan's Lantern* #26, copyright © 1988 by Mike Resnick.

"Kirinyaga" originally appeared in the *Magazine of Fantasy and Science Fiction*, copyright © 1988 by The Mercury Press.

"For I Have Touched the Sky" originally appeared in the *Magazine of Fantasy and Science Fiction*, copyright © 1989 by The Mercury Press.

"On Ice Cubes and Ladies Underwear" originally appeared in *Pulsar* #13, copyright © 1989 by Mike Resnick.

"The End of the Game" originally appeared in somewhat different form as a chapter in *Paradise*, copyright © 1989 by Mike Resnick.

"Digging the Tombs" originally appeared in *Lan's Lantern* #31, copyright © 1989 by Mike Resnick.

Book design by Jack L. Chalker; typesetting by The Mirage Press, Ltd., Westminster, MD; the type is Adobe New Century Schoolbook. The publisher would like to thank Andrew Morrow, whose short-deadline solutions to certain layout problems was essential.

WSFA Press logo by Joe Mayhew.

Printed and bound in the United States of America by Thompson-Shore, Inc., Dexter, MI.

ISBN 0-9621725-1-0

To Carol, as always,

And to Eva Whitley and Jack Chalker,
who would like it if they tried it.

Contents

THROUGH DARKEST RESNICK
WITH GUN AND CAMERA

WHY AFRICA?

I wrote this article at the request of Timothy Lane, editor of Hugo-nominated Fosfax—and when it came time to assemble the pieces for this book, it occurred to me that it would make the perfect introduction.

There is quite a strong body of opinion that the most fascinating alien society ever to appear in a work of fiction is neither Frank Herbert's Dune nor Doc Smith's Civilization nor Isaac Asimov's Foundation, but rather James Clavell's medieval Japan of *Shogun.*

Which is just another way of saying that you needn't look parsecs away for your science fictional source material.

More and more these days, people have stopped asking me "Where do you get those crazy ideas?" and have taken to asking me, "Why Africa?"

This is a shame, because "Africa" has become my answer to the first question.

I don't know when I first became enamoured of Africa—maybe it came from reading Tarzan books, or perhaps watching Disney's "The African Lion" when I was nine years old—but whatever the impetus, I have been collecting every book on Africa that I could get my hands on for the better part of 35 years now (my African library is *much* larger and more valuable than my not-inconsiderable science fiction collection.) I have been a member of the East African and South African and Okavango Wildlife Societies since before I was old enough to vote, and I have volunteered both my writing and my money to several African causes.

But it wasn't until the last decade that I realized that my relationship with the Dark Continent needn't be all give and no take, and that there was more story material there than I could use—even science fictionally—in half a dozen lifetimes. You want an alien society? Forget about Mesklin and Barsoom, and turn your eyes to Kenya.

Here is a modern, 20th-Century nation, totally capitalistic, with two bustling international airports, its very own metropolis (Nairobi, population 1.5 million), and a number of sophisticated industries.

But not a single one of Kenya's 40-plus tribes had a word for "wheel" in 1900.

Not one of them entered the 20th Century with a written language.

90% of the population claims to be Christian, but 80% see their witch doctor far more often than their minister or priest.

80% of all Kenyans of both sexes still undergo circumcision ceremonies as teenagers.

English is the official language of Kenya; less than 5% of the population can speak it.

You think you can't transfer that society to Planet X and get a couple of serious extrapolations out of it?

Or try Uganda. Everybody knows about Idi Amin—but how many people know that Dr. Milton Obote, who succeeded him, killed even more Ugandans than Amin? Or that General Okello, who overthrew Obote, also murdered more of his own countrymen than Amin?

What kind of society, once considered "the pearl of Africa" by no less a statesman than Winston Churchill, can produce three such genocidal maniacs in succession?

How can there *not* be a science fiction novel or two in a society that continually lines up to be slaughtered by its own leaders?

South Africa: A white minority practicing *apartheid* on a continent where its 44 closest neighbors are ruled by their black majorities. You think you can't translate *that* into a grim novel of human xenophobia in a galaxy where we're outnumbered hundreds to one?

How about Tanzania? Here's a country run by perhaps the most brilliant socialist philosopher of this century, Jules Nyerere, whose greatest tragedy is that he didn't have a better country to practice with. No matter what innovation he tried, no matter what lever he pulled, his country was just too poor and barren to respond to his vision, and in the end he bankrupted it, putting the final financial nail in the coffin by being the only leader on the continent who was willing to oppose Idi Amin.

Hard science, soft science, politics, human tragedy—what more could a science fiction writer want than a world drawn from Tanzania?

So I started carving out chunks of the African landscape and finding ways to use them in my science fiction.

Bits and pieces appeared here and there. Chapter 5 of *The Soul Eater* was a hunt for alien beasts, set in a thinly-disguised analog of Tanzania's Ngorongoro Crater. The protagonist was named for an old-time African trader, and the bartender for a Zulu chieftain.

My next novel, *Birthright: The Book of Man*, had a chapter set in the Serengeti Plains.

Nobody screamed foul, so I continued borrowing little parts of Africa for the *Tales Of The Galactic Midway* series and for *Santiago*.

Finally I decided it was time to take the plunge and borrow more than a little bit here and a little bit there.

My first attempt was *Adventures*, a parody of every bad pulp story and B movie ever set on the Dark Continent.

Then came *The Dark Lady*, in which the story had nothing to do with Africa, but was told by an alien who had to function in a xenophobic human society, courtesy of P. Botha and his henchmen. Then I wrote *Ivory*, in which I took an historical artifact—the record tusks of the Kilimanjaro Elephant, who was killed under mysterious circumstances in 1898—and created an epic that spanned eight millennia.

Then came *Paradise*, which is an allegory of Kenya's history from 1890 to 2010.

And continuing over the next few years in *F&SF* and *Asimov's* will be the "Kirinyaga" stories, which chronicle the attempts, as told by an old witch doctor, to preserve a traditional Kikuyu society in the face of 21st Century technology. Five novelets and novellas have already been written; there will be five more.

All different, all reasonably successful with the critics and the readers, and all drawn from a single source: Africa.

I don't write exclusively about Africa, of course; many of my books and stories have nothing to do with it at all. But I truly believe that the ones that have drawn, in whole or in part, upon Africa for inspiration and material constitute my most powerful writings...and, of course, as long as I continue to use it as a source, the IRS tends to look with some favor upon my almost yearly safaris.

They are wonderful experiences, those safaris. There is nothing to match a drive through the savannah, observing everything from huge herds of elephant to the sleek, silent leopard stalking its prey, then returning to camp for a cold drink, a hot dinner, and an evening of listening to old-time hunters and colonists tell their stories while a few yards away lions cough and hyenas giggle in the darkness.

I've never come back from Africa without at least one new novel and a couple of short stories to be written. They can come from seeing an enormous pair of tusks, or a Kikuyu woman carrying eighty pounds of wood on her back while her unencumbered husband walks imperiously ahead of her, or from the crowded streets of Lamu or Cairo, or the "whites only" signs in Cape Town, or even from reading the tombstones in the Railway Cemetery in Nairobi. So I come back to the original question: Why Africa?

The answer is simple: It's more beautiful, more savage, more evocative, and certainly more alien than Mars or Proxima Centauri III.

I'm just glad Clavell visited Asia first, and left Africa for me.

THE LOST RACE

It was while videotaping the Ursula Andress movie, SHE, for a friend that I decided that somebody ought to try to be that funny on purpose. That night I created Lucifer Jones and outlined Adventures, *which takes place from 1922 to 1926 and is a parody of every bad pulp story and B movie ever set in Africa. Writing it was the most fun I ever had at a typewriter. This particular chapter was my answer to Ursula and her buddies.*

You know, diamonds are a lot harder to find than you might think.

I must have spent the better part of two weeks looking in caves and gorges and riverbeds and valleys and abandoned rock quarries without finding a single one. I even checked out a couple of exotic-looking orchards, just in case I was dead wrong about where diamonds came from, but I finally had to admit that there was more to the diamond-prospecting business than met the eye. Since I was fresh out of funds (actually, there's wasn't nothing *fresh* about it—I'd been out of funds for quite a long time), I took a job dealing faro when I hit Germiston, a quaint little village a couple of miles east of Johannesburg. I gave it up after a couple of days, thought, after I earned enough money to buy a second-hand Chautauqua tent.

I supplemented my meager preaching income by hosting a few friendly games of bingo until I realized that the bingo cards were costing me more than I was winning from the natives, since there wasn't much of a market for boers' teeth and such other trinkets as they used for legal tender, and finally I made up my mind to light out for Nairobi the next day to see if I couldn't scare up a little more money in British East Africa than I was finding in the Down Under side of the continent.

I told my helpers to show up at noon for their severance pay, but then I got to thinking about the story of Job and decided that a little hardship and disappointment was probably just the kind of strengthening and hardening their spirits needed, so I turned in early and made up my mind to leave town a bit before daybreak. I was snoring away in my hotel room, minding my own business and not bothering no one, when I was awakened by the sound of a door opening.

I sat up, rubbed my eyes, and saw as pretty a little lady as I had ever experienced standing in my doorway. She was dressed all in blue silks and veils that didn't hide half as much as she thought they did, and she had the strangest headdress topping her yellow hair.

"Have you got it?" she whispered, walking into the room and closing the door behind her.

"Ma'am," I said with a smile, "I've got *it*, and to spare. To what do I owe the distinct pleasure of this here nocturnal visitation?"

"The Malaloki armband," she said. "Where is it?"

"Probably in Malaloki, wherever that may be," I answered. "However, you're welcome to search every inch of me, which I'm sure you'll agree is a pretty generous offer to make to a total stranger."

"But you *must* have it!" she hissed.

"I don't know what you're talking about," I answered.

"You *are* Lucifer Jones, are you not?"

"The Right Reverend Lucifer Jones at your service," I said. "You *sure* you don't want to search me for this here armband?"

"This is not a matter for levity," she said sternly.

"Neither is breaking and entering," I pointed out. "Though," I added, "the Lord does teach us to forgive our brother's trespasses. Of course, He don't say much about our sister's trespasses, but I'm sure you and me can work something out if we just put our heads together."

"I will ask you one more time: Where is it?"

"I don't know," I said with a shrug. "On the other hand, I sure am glad that you've asked me for the last time. What would you like to talk about now?"

She looked at me, frowned, and opened the door, and before I knew it two big white guys dressed in leopardskin robes had burst into the room and were threatening me with spears. They both had on the same kind of headdresses as the girl, kind of feathery with a couple of little jewels right at the front hanging down over their foreheads, but somehow the headdresses didn't look as good on them, or maybe it was just that they kept jabbing me in the short ribs with the points of their weapons.

"I must have that armband, Mister Jones," said the girl.

"*Doctor* Jones," I corrected her, sucking in my stomach as far as I could as the spears kept pressing against it.

"Make no mistake about it, Doctor Jones," she said. "Two men have already died this evening."

"I hope it wasn't nothin' catching," I said with as much compassion as I could muster, which truth to tell wasn't near as much as I might have had under other circumstances.

"They died because of the Malaloki armband," she said meaningfully.

"What is it—some kind of wrestling hold?" I asked.

"An ancient and sacred ornament of the Malaloki, which may be worn only by one of our gods."

"Well, I hate to disappoint a lovable little lady like yourself," I said, "but despite my handsome and clean-cut good looks, I ain't no god."

"The Malaloki armband was stolen two moons past by a disloyal subject," she continued impassively. "We traced it to Germiston, and here we lost it—until tonight. The man who had stolen it had traded it for food and other worldly goods, the storekeeper had sold it to a Boer, the Boer had given it to a black house servant, and the servant lost it to you in a game of chance. You have it, and now you must give it to us or your life shall be forfeit."

"But I ain't seen any armbands!" I said as they began prodding me a little harder with their spear tips. "Not gold nor silver nor brass nor any kind."

"*Wait!*" she commanded, holding her hand imperiously above her head, and suddenly the two guys with the weapons backed off a bit. "Possibly you do not as yet know the shape and texture of that about which I speak. The Malaloki armband has no commercial value, but is made of shells joined together in a mystic design of overwhelming power and import."

"Well, why didn't you say so in the first place?" I said. "I took in what I thought was a little ankle bracelet made of strung-together shells."

"The *armband!*" she exclaimed, finally showing some emotion, even if not the kind I would have preferred to see from a blonde in a see-through blue wraparound.

"I think it's worthless, you think it's priceless," I said. "How's about we split the difference and I trade it to you for a couple of them jewels off your headdresses, unless they got some special religious significance too?"

"Doctor Jones," she said, "we will trade you your life for the armband. That should constitute a considerable profit for you."

"Considering the alternative, I suppose I could do a mite worse," I admitted begrudgingly.

"Where is it?"

"I've got a whole bag of junk—begging your pardon—over at my tent. Wait'll I get my clothes on, and I'll take you there." Which I did, though we must have made a funny-looking sight stalking through the narrow streets of Germiston at three in the morning. I couldn't see much sense returning to the hotel just to wake the desk clerk, so I slipped a deck of cards into my pocket and made up my mind to head right off for Nairobi once our business was done.

When we got to the tent it turned out that none of us had any matches, so I just started walking around, kind of feeling blindly for the bag. After a couple of minutes I stepped on something that made a pretty loud crunching sound, and I knew that I had found the trinket.

The girl ran over and started pulling stuff out of the bag, and a couple of seconds later she gave out a shriek that would have woke such dead as weren't otherwise occupied at the time.

"What seems to be the problem, ma'am?" I asked out of an innate sense of courtesy.

"It's broken!" she cried, holding up a bunch of busted shells that were hanging together by a few torn threads.

"That's a shame," I said sympathetically. "Maybe you could hunt up some clams or oysters or something and stitch up a replacement."

"You do not understand what this means," she wept.

"Maybe even lobster shells," I added thoughtfully. "There's a pretty good seafood shop over in Johannesburg, and..."

"Silence!" roared one of the two men, pointing his spear at me.

I didn't see much sense in making helpful suggestions if that was the way they had been taught to respond to an act of Christian goodwill, so I just stood there while the three of them went into a little pow-wow. Finally they broke it up and the girl walked over to me.

"You will come with us," she announced.

"I really had other plans," I said, and started telling her about how I aimed to build the Tabernacle of Saint Luke. I got about three sentences into my story when one of the men started jabbing me with his spear again.

"You will come with us," she repeated. "You will speak to our gods and tell them how the armband came to be broken, and possibly they will spare our lives."

I took another close look at all their various jewels, which sure seemed pretty common and unimportant to them, and made up my mind on the spot. "I'll be happy to come along with you," I said with a great big smile. "You may not know it, but speaking to gods is one of the very best things I do, me being a man of the cloth and all."

We stepped out of the tent and began walking to the north. After we had gotten a couple of miles out of town, the girl turned to me again.

"I hope you understand, Doctor Jones," she said, "that any attempt to escape while we make our way to Malaloki will be dealt with severely."

"I give you my word as a Christian and a gentleman that such a thought ain't never crossed my mind," I said truthfully, naturally assuming that such a verbal contract expired once we got to wherever they kept their jewels.

Well, we walked and we walked and then we walked some more. I kept assuming that Cairo or Marrakech would pop into view any second, but she assured me that we were still in South Africa, and that we weren't heading no farther than Nyasaland, which I hadn't never heard of before, and which I now began picturing as a great huge field of grass with a bunch of baby nyasas hopping around on it.

During our trek I learned that her name was Melora, and that she had learned her English from some missionaries, which was kind of surprising because it seemed like everyone I had met in Africa had learned their English from missionaries and yet I was the only bonafide missionary that I knew of wandering around in the bush. She surprised me still further by saying that her native tongue wasn't French or German or Portugese or anything like that, but was the Malaloki dialect, which was the first time I learned that they invented languages as well as armbands.

We were about ten days into our little journey when we crossed into Nyasaland. The landscape started changing, and pretty soon the bushland turned into a kind of gently rolling forest filled with gently rolling rhinos and leopards and other fearsome beasts that looked like the wanted nothing more than a little snack made of Christian missionary and maybe a little bit of blonde Malaloki for dessert, but our two big spearmen managed to bluff all the animals away, which was undoubtedly for the best since I couldn't see how they could reload a spear if their first fling missed, and we passed through the forest unscathed except for tick bites and mosquito bites and fly bites and being bothered by some rude maribou storks that kept flying overhead right after they'd had lunch, and finally we came to a great big volcanic crater stuck right in the middle of a long plateau.

I figured that we were going to hike around it, but Melora walked straight ahead and started following a narrow little path up the side of it. I grabbed hold of her arm and explained that while the top of the crater was undoubtedly a good sight closer to God and Heaven, she didn't have to do this on my account, as I was perfectly content to worship Him from afar, or at least ground level, for a few more years, and besides the path disappeared a couple of hundred yards ahead of us.

For a woman with a short little nose, she sure made a production of looking down it at me. Finally she yanked her arm loose and started climbing again. I called ahead to her that I was going to start back down to the base of the volcano and would meet her on the other side, but no sooner were the words out of my mouth than the two big guys started jabbing me with their spears again, so I didn't have no choice but to follow her.

I did so for maybe a hundred yards when suddenly she just upped and vanished. I mean, one second I was following that beautiful round bottom up the path, which in truth was all the kept me going, and the next second she was gone, beautiful bottom and all. I stopped, scratched my head, and looked around, but couldn't see hide nor hair of her, which was a considerable amount of hide and hair to vanish from the earth all at once. Then I felt a hand on my arm, and I was dragged off the path into a narrow little tunnel.

"Where are we?" I whispered.

"Just follow me," said Melora.

"Follow you?" I repeated. "I can't even *see* you."

"Grab my hand," she said.

I reached out for it.

"*That*, Doctor Jones, is *not* my hand."

I apologized, and after a little more groping around I finally got ahold of what I was supposed to get ahold of, and pretty soon we were wending our way through this damp, winding tunnel. After about ten minutes of walking into walls and into Melora, who may have been softer than the walls but wasn't a whole lot friendlier or more understanding, we emerged onto a large ledge overlooking a village on the grassy floor of the dead volcano.

"Malaloki?" I asked.

She nodded. A little river wended its way amongst the thatched huts, then went out through a hole it had carved out of one of the walls. This crater didn't hold a candle to some of the larger ones I was aware of, like for instance the Ngorongoro Crater in Tanganyika, but on the other hand the Ngorongoro Crater wasn't awash in jewels and blonde women, so I didn't feel no great disappointment with my current surroundings.

Melora waited until the two big guys had joined us, then led the way down another winding trail to the base of the wall.

A bunch of white women wearing even less than Melora raced up and jabbered at her in some foreign tongue. She talked right back at them, just as quick and incomprehensible, and took me by the hand and led me through the village until we came to the biggest hut, which was located smack-dab in the center. Then she bowed and backed away.

In front of the hut were two grass hammocks, and in each hammock was a grubby-looking white man with a bushy beard. One of them must have been close to seven feet tall, and the other couldn't have been more than an inch or two over five feet. Both of them were wearing khaki pants that had been cut off above the knees, and they each had a batch of necklaces made out of emeralds and sapphires and rubies and other colorful baubles.

"Well, look what we got here, brother," said the big one.

"Sure as hell don't look like no Malaloki I ever seen," said the little one.

"What's your name, stranger?" asked the big one.

"The Honorable Right Reverend Doctor Lucifer Jones at your service," I said, stooping over in a courtly bow. "Begging your pardon, but you gents sure don't sound like Malalokis from what little I've heard you speak."

"Neither do you," said the little one.

"No reason why I should," I said. "I'm an American."

"So are we," said the big one.

"Of course," added the little one, "we're also gods, but around these here parts the two ain't necessarily incompatible."

"In fact," continued the big one, "along with being gods and Americans, we're also brothers. I'm Frothingham Schmidt and he's Oglethorpe Schmidt, but them who would consider themselves our friends, or at least express an interest in ever seeing another sunrise, call us Long Schmidt and Short Schmidt."

"I'm Short Schmidt," said the little one.

"Well, I'm mighty glad to find a couple of countrymen here," I said. "You wouldn't happen to have a little something for a thirsty traveler, with maybe just enough alcohol to whip the tar out of the germs?"

"First things first," said Long Schmidt. "We ain't set foot outside our little kingdom in six years, and we got some important questions to ask about the rest of the world."

"And well you should," I said. "You'll be pleased and happy to know that we won the War to End All Wars."

"Who gives a damn about that?" said Short Schmidt. "We're Pittsburgh boys, Pittsburgh born and bred. Where did the Pirates finish last year?"

"Third or fourth, as I recollect," I answered.

"*Damn* that John McGraw!" said Long Schmidt. "Tell me, Doctor Jones—who won the Kentucky Derby of 1917?"

"Seems to me that it was Omar Khayyam," I said.

"Yahoo!" cried Short Schmidt, tossing a necklace into the air. "If we ever get back to Casey's Bar, old Flathead Mahoney is gonna owe me a double sawbuck!"

"We didn't mean to forget our manners, Doctor Jones," said Long Schmidt. "It's just that certain things are very important to us. Now we'll join you in that drink." He clapped his hands twice, and a couple of ripe young maidens brought us a round of fruit drinks, with just a little something extra added.

"So, Doctor Jones," said Short Schmidt when we had all had a couple of long swallows, "what brings you to the kingdom of the Malaloki?"

"Friendship, curiosity, an adventurous spirit, and mostly a woman named Melora," I said.

"Ah, yes, Melora," said Short Schmidt. "Lovely girl."

"Our wife," added Long Schmidt.

"One of 'em, anyway," said Short Schmidt. "Truth to tell, Jones, the blasted village is damned near over-flowing with goddesses-by-marriage."

"Easy now, brother," said Long Schmidt. "Doctor Jones is a man of the cloth. Perhaps he disapproves."

"No such a thing," I assured them. "Solomon had a pile of wives, and the Good Book never said a word against him."

"Doctor Jones," said Short Schmidt with a smile, "you got the makings of a right friendly neighbor."

"Thank you kindly," I said. "You fellers mind if I ask you a couple of questions?"

"Go right ahead," said Short Schmidt.

"Who are the Malaloki, and how'd you ever get to be gods here?"

"Well, that's kind of a long story, Doctor Jones," said Long Schmidt. "Me and Short came over to Africa seven years ago to scare us up some diamonds. Didn't seem that hard when we planned it, but I'll be damned if we could find a single one."

"Diamond mines is well hid in these parts," I agreed.

"*Mines?*" exclaimed Short Schmidt. "Son of a bitch! We thought they grew inside oysters!"

"That's pearls," I said. "Did you find any of them, at least?"

"Never even found an oyster," said Short Schmidt. "Came near to getting et by crocodiles a couple of times."

"Oh," I said. "Well, if you ever go oyster hunting again, I think you'll have a little more luck in the ocean than in the rivers."

"We ain't likely to ever see a ocean again," said Long Schmidt mournfully. "Let me get back to the main thrust of our tragic story, Doctor Jones, so you'll know why we're so happy to see you."

"Be my guest," I said, taking another drink that one of the local maidens offered me.

"Like Short told you, we came here to seek fame and fortune, mostly the latter. Matter of fact, we had a little more fame with the local constabularies than we could handle, which is how we came to take our leave of the civilized portions of Africa and head inland."

"We set up shop as traders," added Short Schmidt. "We'd make a round of the Zulus, swapping brass cartridges for goats. Then we'd trade the goats for salt, trade the salt for cattle, and sell the cattle at market. It was a tidy little business."

"So what happened?" I asked.

"Well, we had a little difference of opinion with a tribe called the Shona about whether having a couple of friendly drinks and smokes together constitutes a bonafide proposition of marriage, and we had to take our leave of them a little more quickly than we would have liked."

"Perfectly understandable," I said.

"My thoughts precisely," said Long Schmidt. "I just wish the Shona could have seen it that way. Anyway, we took off in the middle of the night, and since our bushcraft ain't exactly up to snuff, especially by Shona standards, we kept on running for two days and two nights, just to make sure that we weren't being followed too closely."

"And on the third morning," continued Short Schmidt, "we ran up against this here crater. We were both feeling kind of tired and out of sorts, what with having been running for our lives all that time, so we thought we'd climb up the wall of the crater a way and take a little rest once we were out of sight. Well, we stumbled onto some tunnel or other, and an hour later here we were, surrounded by the lost tribe of the Malaloki."

"Of course, they ain't so lost as they was," added Long Schmidt, "with both of us and now you stumbling

"Well, truth to tell," said Short Schmidt, "there seems to be a fine and highly technical legal line between the two. Seems that their legends told of a couple of gods who would come here disguised as white men."

"Well, you got no problem that I can see," I said

"Hah!" snorted Long Schmidt.

"The problem," said Short Schmidt, "is that two *other* white guys wandered in here about fifty years ago, and after they'd got all the ladies pregnant and picked up the choicer gemstones, they just up and left."

"So the Malaloki have decided that as long as we stay here we must be gods, and we can do damned near anything we want," continued Long Schmidt. "But the second we leave, we've proved that we're just men after all, and they've got about twenty beefy young men on the other side of that crater wall waiting to make pincushions out of us."

"I can see where that might get to be a nuisance," I agreed. "That's why we sent Melora after you," said Short Schmidt. "By the way," I said, "I'm supposed to tell you that Melora didn't break the sacred armband. I kind of stomped on it accidentally."

"'Tain't noways sacred anyhow," said Short Schmidt. "We knew that one of the young bucks was going to Germiston for some seeds to plant, so we snuck it into his pouch and told Melora that he'd went and swiped a sacred object."

"How come?" I asked.

"Melora ain't exactly the most humorous critter we've ever run into," said Long Schmidt. "We figured she'd move heaven and earth to get that armband back, and we were kind of hoping that she'd wipe out enough locals so that someone would follow her back here, like maybe an army or something big like that."

"So while we're delighted to see a fellow countryman, and especially one who knows how the Pirates are doing these days," said Short Schmidt, "I'd locals so that someone would follow her back here, like maybe an army or something big like that."

"So while we're delighted to see a fellow countryman, and especially one who knows how the Pirates are doing these days," said Short Schmidt, "I'd have to say that on the whole you represent a considerable disappointment to us, meaning no offense."

"None taken," I said. "Who *are* the Malaloki, anyway?"

"As near as we can figure it," said Long Schmidt, "they're the descendants of some Roman outpost. Probably been living in the crater some fifteen hundred years or so. A few of 'em leave every now and then to buy things we can't get down here and to learn a little English, but they always come back. For a while there me and Short really talked up the outside world in the hope that one by one they'd all go out and make their way and leave us alone here with the jewels, but so far it ain't happened."

"So here we are," concluded Short Schmidt, "gods of the Malaloki, with the power of life and death over our subjects and every whim catered to—so long as we don't walk more than six hundred yards from where we are now. We may never see the Pirates again!"

"Power of life and death, you say?" I asked.

"We're gods, ain't we?"

"Why not kill 'em off and just walk out free as birds?" I suggested."

"We've thunk it over long and hard," admitted Short Schmidt. "But while we don't back off none at a little serious swindling and cardsharking, murdering a whole lost tribe would probably put us off our feed."

"Of course, we may eventually get around to killing off all the menfolk," added Long Schmidt. "I don't like the way they look at us whenever we get married, which is pretty damned often now that I come to think of it."

"Well, now, brothers," I said, "you sound right happy and fulfilled as things stand. What in the world would you do if you ever got out of here?"

"Run like hell," said Short Schmidt devoutly.

"I mean after that," I said.

"See if we couldn't land us a grubstake and marry us a couple of good women and settle down, making sure to buy lifetime season tickets to the Pirates. Is old Honus Wagner still playing for them?"

"He quit five or six years back, as I recollect," I said.

"Damn!" said Short Schmidt. "No wonder they ain't won any pennants to speak of."

"*Damn* that John McGraw and his Giants!" added Long Schmidt passionately.

I could see they were bound and determined to talk about baseball for a few hours, so I decided that it was a good time to take my leave of them. "Well," I said, "this has been a fascinating experience, hobnobbing with a couple of flesh-and-blood gods and seeing a lost civilization and all, but I think maybe the time has come for me to depart."

"What makes you think *you're* going anywhere?" demanded Long Schmidt.

"What reason have you got to keep me?" I said. "I told you everything I know about baseball, and nobody's got around to declaring me a god yet."

"First you got to help us get out of here," said Short Schmidt. "After all, fair is fair."

"I don't see nothing fair about it," I said, getting a little hot under the collar.

"Don't look so glum, Jones," said Long Schmidt. "If you actually *do* figure a way to get us out of here, we'll let you scoop up a handful of gems on the way out."

Which of course put a whole new light on things.

I let one of their wives lead me to a little hut, and I lay down in a hammock and divided my attention between her and the problem at hand, spending most of the night tackling first one and then the other. And by morning I had the solution.

I hunted up Melora, who was about as giggly as ever, which is to say not at all, and told her that I had hit upon a way to turn her gods and husbands into a pair of contented stay-at-homes. "Truly?" she said, her eyes widening.

"Trust me," I said confidently.

"It is almost too much to ask."

"It all depends on you, Melora," I told her.

"What must I do?" she asked.

"I want you to pick up a couple of rubies or emeralds from wherever it is you guys are hiding them, and then go on a little shopping trip to Germiston for me."

I had to explain what I wanted two or three times before she finally understood, and I told her to make sure to take a couple of husky lads along to haul my purchase back.

Then, after she left sometime around noon, I brought out the Good Book and decided to see if I couldn't bring a little of the true religion to these white heathen and get them to cast their false gods out into the cold, just in case my other idea didn't work.

Well, I was at it for the better part of three weeks and no one got converted, but we all had a fine old time singing hymns and trying to live up to the doings and deeds of all them holy men, especially in regard to all the begatting they did.

The Malaloki were fair to middling cooks, and were the first of Roman descent I'd run across who didn't smother everything in tomatoes and mozzarella cheese. The Schmidt brothers had shown them how to make a kind of wine from fermented fruits that didn't taste too good but packed one hell of a punch, and between the eating and the drinking and the begatting I sure couldn't see why they were so all-fired eager to leave.

Twenty days after Melora left she returned, with her two companions lugging a batch of packages. I had them put the stuff into my hut before the brothers saw them, and went to work. When I was done assembling everything, I made sure it all worked and then called Long Schmidt and Short Schmidt over.

"What have you got to show us, Jones?" said Long Schmidt, ducking his head down to get in through my doorway.

"Looks kind of like a radio," said Short Schmidt.

"Shortwave," I said.

"Should that mean something?" asked Long Schmidt.

I held the earphones between them and started cranking the dynamo.

"The Pirates lead two to nothing in the seventh, and John McGraw is calling Heinie Groh back and is sending Frankie Frisch up to pinch-hit with runners on first and—"

I pulled a tube out of the set and smashed it on the floor of the hut.

"My God!" wailed Short Schmidt. "What have you done?"

"Nothing much," I said pleasantly. "I got a spare hidden away."

"Where?" screamed Long Schmidt in agonized tones.

"Why, if I told you, it wouldn't be hidden much longer, would it?" I asked.

"Fix it!" screamed Short Schmidt.

"It's *my* radio," I said. "I put it together and I attached it to the dynamo and I even laid six hundred feet of antenna up the side of the crater. I'll fix it when I feel like listening to it again. Right now, though, I'm planning on taking a nap."

"We'll kill you!" bellowed Long Schmidt, tears streaming down his bearded face.

"That ain't going to get you your tube," I said.

"What do you want for it?" said Short Schmidt, getting down on his knees and sobbing a little.

"Oh, nothing much," I answered. "Maybe just my freedom and a handful of gemstones to tide me over during hard times."

"That was to be your reward for getting us out of here," said Long Schmidt accusingly.

"Why not think over your position for a minute?" I said. "You got more wives than you can shake a stick at, you got a couple of cushy lifetime jobs with no heavy lifting, and you got the Pittsburgh Pirates just a couple of huts away. You got more precious stones than anyone ever thought existed, and nice weather, and three squares a day. Are you sure you really *want* to leave?"

They put their heads together and muttered under their breaths for a while. Then Short Schmidt walked over to his own hut and returned a minute later with a big metal box.

"One handful," he said, opening it up. "No more."

I reached in and pulled out a fistful of rubies and sapphires and other such trinkets and stuffed them into my pockets. Then I took them out behind my hut to a little spot I'd marked, dug down about five or six inches with my fingers, and handed them the tube.

"Anything I can do for you two when I reach civilization?" I asked, preparing to take my leave of them while they were fiddling with the shortwave. "Any messages you want me to deliver?"

"Just send a note to our folks back in Pittsburgh telling them we're okay," said Short Schmidt. "And maybe find a way to tell the Pirates they need more left-handed pitching."

Just then the Giants score three runs in the top of the eighth, and I could see that there wasn't much sense in trying to talk to them any longer, as they were spending all their energy calling down their godly wrath on John McGraw, so I took my leave of them.

Melora shot me the first smile I had ever seen from her and walked me to the tunnel and guided me through and didn't even holler when I didn't exactly grab her hand again.

We finally made it to the plateau that the crater sat on. I kissed her good-bye real courtly-like and, with a handsome fortune in my pockets, I set off for civilization with the happy knowledge that me and God would finally be co-landlords of the Tabernacle of Saint Luke.

STALKING THE PERFECT SAFARI

To amortize my first safari, I sold this piece on the advantages of having a private guide to about a dozen local newspapers and magazines. Four years later, it's still on file in the Travel section of the Delphi Computer Network.

Maybe it was Teddy Roosevelt's fault. Perhaps Edgar Rice Burroughs was to blame. Possibly it was one of those magnificent Disney documentaries. But whatever the reason, I had spent most of my life wanting to take a safari to Africa while there was still some wilderness left to see.

So, when my publisher recently offered me a contract for a science fiction novel set in East Africa, I decided that the time had finally come to make the pilgrimage, especially since the I.R.S. might look upon such a trip with some compassion.

Then began a search for the Perfect Safari. I wrote off to some 25 companies specializing in package tours, and when the last of their brochures had arrived, I was *still* searching. Somehow I just didn't want to spend my dream vacation crammed into a minibus with a dozen other Americans, most of whom would rather be watching the Cowboys playing the Redskins. I didn't want to be led around by a social director, but by an experienced guide who knew Africa as well as Pete Rose knows the way to first base, and I began to get the sinking feeling that such safaris existed only in the movies and in the writings of early explorers and hunters. Then one day I saw a two-line classified ad in the back of a small-circulation nature magazine. It promised individually-tailored safaris in which the client and his party chose their own locations (no "three unscheduled shopping days in beautiful downtown Balguda, *pop. 374*"), selected their own lodgings (no "authentic African campsights" in mosquito-infested swamps), and shared their guide and his vehicle with no one.

Which was how I met Perry Mason—not the fictional lawyer, but the real-life ex-white-hunter and safari guide.

Perry had been sent to Kenya during the Mau Mau emergency, fell in love with the country, and stayed to become a white hunter. When hunting was outlawed in 1977, most hunters returned to their native lands or headed off to neighboring African countries where hunting was still permitted, but Perry and a handful of others, still passionately enamoured of Kenya, decided to remain right where they were and put their knowledge of the bush to work as independent photographic safari guides.

It sounded intriguing, and the more I queried him, the better I liked his notion of a safari. His clients (which have recently included a professor of ornithology, a butterfly collector, and a couple of professional photographers) consult with him directly (P.O. Box 49655, Nairobi, Kenya) or his American agent (Sherry Corbett, P.O. Box 1643, Darien, CT. 08620) and then create their own itineraries. Perry will overrule them only if a particular lodge or camp or park is not currently up to his high standards. As for price, no trip that takes you halfway around the world can be termed inexpensive, but we were amazed to find that the typical independent guide's fee was only about 20% more than most package tours charge—and we made most of it back by purchasing discount airfares, whereas almost all the package tours are tied into air charter rates that cost much more. So Perry added a novelist to his list of clients, and off my wife and I went in early February, hoping that the safari would live up to our expectations.

In point of fact, it exceeded them.

We saw the huge game herds of the Masai Mara, and the snows atop Mount Kenya and Mount Kilimanjaro, and the spectacular birdlife along the Rift Valley lakes, and the twisting streets in the truly exotic cities of Mombasa and Lamu, and the stark, savage beauty of the Northern Frontier District, and the hidden waterfalls high up in the Aberdare Mountains. We saw the elephants of Tsavo, and the hippos of Mzima Springs, and the lions of Amboseli, and the leopards of Maralal. We went far off the beaten path to visit those locations I had to examine as part of the research for my novel. And we began and ended our safari at Nairobi's historic Norfolk Hotel, where Teddy Roosevelt and Ernest Hemingway and Robert Ruark had begun and ended *their* safaris. And, from almost the moment we arrived, the advantages of our personalized safari were made manifest to us. We had been scheduled to spend our fourth and fifth night in Kenya at the famous Samburu River Lodge. At the last moment Perry had changed our reservations to the totally *un*-famous Buffalo Springs tented camp about 30 miles away—and while 250 package tourists looked out from the Samburu Lodge across a river bed that had dried up the week before and wondered where all the game had gone, we joined some 18 other visitors at Buffalo Springs (most of them with their own knowledgable private guides) and practically had to shag elephants out of our path on the way to the dining room. Tourists would come into our camp in the Mara, grumbling about the absence of big cats, and we would secretly smile to each other, for Perry's bushcraft had gotten us to within 15 yards of a lioness nursing her cubs. Travelers would complain about the lack of anything to do at night, while we would visit with Perry's friends, who would regale us for hours with fascinating stories about the days when Kenya was still a frontier. Diners would think they were ordering fish and get beef (or vice versa), while we would simply tell Perry what we wanted and he would translate it into perfect Swahili. Groups would come in stiff and sore from riding in cramped minibuses, while we would come in happy and relaxed after sprawling in our oversized 4-wheel-drive safari car.

Even on the safari circuit, the existence of Kenya's independent guides remains one of the tourist industry's best-kept secrets. From time to time we'd pause in a game lodge to compare notes with other tourists, and the story was invariably the same: the few with private guides were having the time of their lives, the multitude with package tours frequently were not—or, perhaps sadder still, they *thought* they were until they spoke to someone with a private guide, compared experiences and prices, and realized what they were missing.

When all is said and done, there are a lot of ways to visit the cities and game parks of Kenya. A few hardy souls go it alone, and come face-to-face with some of the problems involved in visiting a Third World nation: unfamiliar languages and customs, unpaved and unmarked roads, different currencies, and very little source material with which to prepare themselves. Most people choose to sign up for a package tour, and some of them are quite satisfied. A handful of us have found a better, more luxurious, and not necessarily more expensive, way, and invite you to consider it.

But not during September of 1987. I've already made my down payment.

WHAT I DID ON MY WINTER VACATION

One day George Laskowski, editor/publisher of the Hugo-winning Lan's Lantern, *asked me for a contribution. I told him that I didn't have anything handy, but that I would be happy to write a diary of my forthcoming safari. He took it...and thus began a tradition that continues to this day.*

February 3, 1986: The safari did not begin auspiciously. In fact, the moment we arrived at the airport fog set in and they shut everything down, which sent me into a momentary panic since we had purchased our New York-to-London and London-to-Nairobi fares at huge but absolutely nonrefundable/nonchangeable discount rates—and if we were more than a couple of hours late getting out of Cincinnati, I was going to have to shell out an extra $5,000 or so to buy brand-new non-discount tickets on later intercontinental flights. The fog finally lifted and the airport re-opened less than five minutes before we were due to take off, and Carol poured what was left of me into a seat.

Eleanor Wood, my literary agent, dropped by Kennedy Airport to visit while we were waiting for the London flight to depart, and also delivered some Italian and Japanese royalties that had just arrived, which helped put me back on a more even emotional keel. We talked about all the sights we were going to see, and when my enthusiasm got out of hand, as it tends to do whenever I discuss East Africa, she tactfully reminded me that I was also (I think her word was *primarily*) going there to research *Ivory*, a long novel I'm scheduled to write during the latter half of 1986.

I explained that we had hired a personal guide who had promised to take us to all the places I had to see for the book, and to introduce us to a number of old-time pioneers and hunters with interesting stories to tell. She looked dubious; writers, after all, are supposed to suffer, not go gallavanting off on luxury safaris.

(Actually, writers are supposed to *write*, but sometimes they just screw around codifying their vacations for *Lan's Lantern*.) The movie on the flight to London was a turkey entitled *Jagged Edge*, a film we were forced to sit through three more times during the next 22 days before finally escaping from the programming director of British Airways. Therefore, I might as well take this opportunity to get even: Jeff Bridges is guilty *guilty* **GUILTY!!!**

(Ah. I feel much better about it now.)

February 4: Actually, I don't remember a hell of a lot about February 4. We landed at London at 8:00 AM, immediately went to an airport hotel, took a nap until our daughter, Laura, who is living in London these days, dropped by to visit in the afternoon, checked out at about 3:30, and climbed aboard the plane to Nairobi at 6:30 PM.

February 5: We landed at the Nairobi airport, were met by Perry Mason (our guide), and drove to the Norfolk Hotel, an elegant old colonial establishment (and the second hotel in the interior of East Africa, dating back to 1906) where such notables in the realm of he-man heroics as Teddy Roosevelt, Ernest Hemingway and Robert Ruark had begun their safaris. The grounds were exquisitely landscaped, with lovely gardens, a pair of aviaries, and a number of historical remnants, such as the first tractor, rickshaw, and automobile in Kenya. (I hadn't even realized that there *were* rickshaws in Africa.) We soon discovered that breakfast and lunch on the safari circuit, without exception, would consist of lavish all-you-can-eat buffets, and had the first of quite a few belt-loosening meals. While Carol unpacked, I paid a visit to the East African Wildlife Society, where I autographed some copies of *Adventures* and sold an article to *Swara*, their official publication.

After lunch, we had Perry drive us to the National Museum, where we saw what are purported to be the world's largest collections of sea shells and butterflies, some fascinating native art and costumes, and the stuffed remains of Ahmed, a bull elephant who carried the heaviest ivory of the past quarter-century or so. Just across street of the museum is the Nairobi Snake and Reptile Park, and we spent a few minutes there. A sign within the enclosure housing a pair of 18-foot-long Nile crocodiles stated that anyone tossing food into the area would be forced to retrieve it personally. (Not surprisingly, the enclosure was spotless.)

Finally, we drove out to Karen Blixen's farmhouse, took a tour of it, and wound up having dinner at the Carnivore, a fabulous open-air restaurant specializing in Africa's wild game meats. We had topi, hartebeest, Uganda kob, and a number of other game animals, and were joined by Tessa Gross, a friend of Perry's who had just finished working on *Out of Africa*, on which she supplied and trained the horses and also tought Meryl Streep to ride.

February 6: We drove north to Thika (where Elspeth Huxley's mother planted her Flame Trees), and spent about an hour hunting for, and finally finding, an area called Fourteen Falls, where (obviously) fourteen waterfalls converge. I'd seen a photo of it some years ago, and had written to Perry that I wanted to visit it. He couldn't find it on any maps, but he had been there some 20 years earlier and knew the general area, and since he speaks fluent Swahili he simply began questioning people in the Thika area until he came up with three men in a row who agreed about where it was—a longer and more difficult task than you might think. (I might add that, once we found it, it was quite lovely and well worth the effort.)

Then we went north past Nyeri into the Aberdare Mountains, and on to the Ark, a game-viewing lodge in the Aberdare National Park, where, from no more than 20 yards away, we saw buffalo, giant forest hogs, hyenas, bushbuck, about 200 different species of birds, and the only rhino we were to see on the entire safari. Perry also introduced us to Ian Hardy, a charming gentleman who had been a white hunter back in the 1930s and spent the evening regaling us with stories of the good old days.

February 7: We left the Ark after breakfast and drove about 20 miles to the Aberdare Country Club, which looks like a clone of Karen Blixen's house. We were given a 5-room cottage for the three of us, left our bags there, and drove into the practically empty park (we were one of only two cars to enter all day). We drove up to a hidden waterfall Perry knew of at 11,000 feet altitude (well, it wasn't *quite* hidden; there was a sign warning us that a female tourist had been eaten by a lion there a month earlier). Anyway, we had lunch, then ascended via 4-wheel-drive to the Queen's Cave waterfall at 13,000 feet. Surprisingly, the altitude didn't affect us at all, at least not while we drove or walked downhill. We did notice that we started panting heavily when we walked up even the slightest incline. We saw some elephants and buffalo, as well as some rare colobus monkeys, and finally returned to our cottage, where we ran into Ian Hardy again. I had asked him some questions about John Boyes, a turn-of-the-century Kenya pioneer and general scalawag whose career I have appropriated, in bits and pieces, in a number of my

novels (and about whom I would like, someday, to write
a biography) and Ian had evidently spent the entire day
hunting up my answers for me.

February 8: We drove through Nanyuki to Mount
Kenya, and checked into the Mount Kenya Safari Club,
where we were given a private two-bedroom cottage,
with oversized sunken showers and tubs and a pair of
fireplaces, that was equal to any suite we've ever stayed
in at the Plaza in New York or the Ritz in London—and
the food was better. We were entertained at lunchtime
by two dozen Chuka dancers, and we spent most of the
afternoon loafing and wandering around the grounds,
which include a putting green, a pool, a bowling green, a
number of ponds for waterbirds, and an animal
orphanage. I also interviewed a couple of Perry's friends
who happened to be at the club, and Carol and I began
putting together some notions for a new novel based on
various aspects of Kenyan history. (By halfway through
the trip I had filled more than 100 pages of my
notebook, and had the book, which will be published in
hardcover and paperback by Tor under the title
Paradise, totally plotted out.)
     I ought to say a little something about Perry while
I'm thinking about it. He came to Kenya in 1952, a
beardless youth of 19, to fight the Mau Mau. He was
given a squad of a dozen Samburu and Wanderobo
warriors and a gun, driven to the Aberdare Mountains
(90% of the Mau Maus were holed up in the Aberdares
and on Mount Kenya), and told to proceed with
anti-terrorist activities. He knew neither the language
nor the geography nor the tactics, but the fact that he's
still alive shows that he picked them up pretty quickly.
In 1956, when the Mau Mau were virtually disbanded,
he became a successful white hunter. Then, when
hunting was outlawed in 1977, he went to his second
love, horses, and was the leading steeplechase jockey in
Kenya in 1978 and 1979, and when he got too heavy to
ride, he was the leading trainer of steeplechase winners

in 1980. He also represented Kenya in the All-Africa pistol-shooting championships on three different occasions. Finally, in 1980, he began a photographic safari business, specializing in ushering individuals and couples through rather idiosyncratic personalized itineraries. (I was his first writer, but he'd been out with two professional photographers, a butterfly collector, and a professor of ornithology within the past year.) We got along famously—in fact, I'm dedicating a book to him—and I soon discovered that he was far better-read than I had expected. All in all, he was an excellent guide and companion (and we've already made a down payment for our next safari, which we'll be taking in September of 1987.)

February 9: We drove north through Isiolo to the Northern Frontier District, the harsh, savage desert country that covers the northern half of Kenya, and wound up at the Buffalo Springs tented camp. (The tents—thank heaven!—weren't the ones I remember from my scouting days; while small, they each had two beds with inner-spring mattresses, a dressing area, and bathrooms with hot and cold running water, flush toilets, and showers.) It was hot—perhaps 105 degrees, and it felt even hotter after three very cool days in the mountains—and we were at the end of the dry season. We took an afternoon game run, and I was amazed to find a herd of more than 100 oryx grazing off a section of ground that I wouldn't have believed could feed a single cow. We ran across gerunuk, reticulated giraffe, and Grevy's zebra, three of the rarest mammals in Africa, and also spent some time observing a huge tribe of baboons and a delightful family of warthogs. It was our first real game run after three days of observing scenery and birds, and we were overwhelmed by the abundance of wildlife Perry was able to find in what is essentially a desert. When we returned to the camp, we found half a dozen elephants placidly grazing some 50 yards away from our tent.

February 10: This is the day we met Jumbo, who will probably remain my favorite African animal. Carol woke me at about 5:30 in the morning to say that there was an enormous bull elephant lying on his side about ten yards from the front of our tent. Elephants don't sleep lying down, I explained while pulling the covers over my head; it would crush their lungs. See for yourself, she replied—and sure enough, there was this mountain of elephant on its side right outside our tent flap. Nothing was moving but his tail, and I spent the better part of an hour standing at the front of the tent, my video camera trained on him, waiting for him to get up and do something. Perry wandered over from his own tent at about 6:30, and explained that the elephant was probably dying, since elephants never lie down once they're fully grown. We were scheduled to spend another night at the camp, and visions of hyenas and vultures fighting over an increasingly odoriferous carcass flashed through my mind (and nose) as we toddled off to breakfast, being careful not to step on old Jumbo as we went. When we returned about half an hour later he was on his feet, placidly grazing about fifty yards away from our tent and obviously unaware of the fact that he was on the brink of death.

While eating breakfast, we queried a number of the other guests about when they had seen. Most were quite negative; except for the half-dozen elephants around the camp, they'd run into a few oryx and a couple of ostrich and that was it. This was the morning we discovered the difference between going out with a white hunter as opposed to a social director. We left on our game run, and just as I was about to express the opinion that even Perry wasn't likely to scare up any animals in this barren environment, he pointed out the window and we saw a herd of about 80 elephants not half a mile away. Perry pulled off the road and began approaching them obliquely, never seeming to be getting any nearer to them, yet within seven or eight minutes we were literally in the middle of them, totally surrounded by some 400 tons of elephant. They paid us scant attention, we got some fabulous footage of the babies playing and nursing—and I never again doubted Perry's ability to find game where none was supposed to exist. In fact, we found about 50 other species on the morning run, and returned, hot but content, for lunch—where we ran into Jumbo again.

He had finished grazing around our tent, and had moved his base of operations over to the restaurant—which, like all Kenyan game lodge bars and restaurants, was an open-air affair. It had a roof to protect us from the sun and rain, but there were no walls, just a two-foot-high stone barrier and a row of shrubs and flowers to outline the area. They were very lovely shrubs and flowers, and they must have smelled as good as they looked, because Jumbo suddenly ambled over and began eating them, not ten feet from where a number of guests were eating their own meals. Now, as friendly as he looked, he was still a large, wild bull elephant, and it was a potentially hazardous situation, so the kitchen staff and the waiters decided to drive him away. They began picking up rocks and hurling them at him from point-blank range. (I have the entire episode on videotape, and you can hear those rocks slamming noisily off his carcass.) Now, Jumbo was no more than eight or ten yards from his tormenters; it would have been no effort for him to take two quick steps and turn them all into jelly. But all he did was eat more and more rapidly, finally ambling off amid a hail of rocks with the very last flower clutched firmly in his trunk. We gave him a standing ovation. Having thoughtfully elected not to play people-pong, he walked over to the waterhole (almost all lodges are built on or near waterholes, so guests can observe the fauna while both they and the animals are busy drinking), and decided to play a game of chicken with a pair of crocodiles who were sunning themselves. The smart money went on Jumbo, and he won in a walk.

That morning Carol had forgotten the first rule of the African wild and drank some tap water, and became violently sick to her stomach. This necessitated her missing the afternoon game run. (We considered dragging her outside and leaving her for the hyenas in traditional African fashion, but since there weren't any hyenas around, we medicated her instead. She recovered eventually, but she was sick on and off for the next 10 days.)

After lunch, while Carol lay in the tent and tried to decide who to cut out of her will, Perry and I drove over to the Samburu River Lodge to fill up the safari car with gas, gas stations not being all that plentiful in the desert. (The lodge is really quite luxurious. We had originally been slated to stay there, and I was a little upset at winding up at Buffalo Springs—but, as always, Perry knew what he was doing. The river that flows by the lodge was totally dry, and all the wildlife was now in the Buffalo Springs area. In fact, one of my great missed photo opportunities centered around a foppish-looking Italian gentleman, dressed in his gold chains and his bikini, standing on the dry river bed and wondering where the hell he could go for a swim.)

February 11: We spent about 4 hours driving from Buffalo Springs to Maralal, which was back at a reasonable altitude—7,000 feet, which meant a temperature in the low 80's—passing through some beautiful if stark landscape as we did so. Maralal is owned by a friend of Perry's, a former hunter, who was a very gracious host and spent quite some time answering my questions. Maralal is not a national park, but a rather private lodge, and we were the only guests there. We sat out on the deck of the lodge for a few hours, drinking Tusker beers (the only kind you can get in most Kenyan locations) and watching hundreds of impala, zebra, warthogs, elands, and vervet monkeys drinking from an artificial water hole that was no more than 20 feet away. Then we carted our bags to our private cabin, a beautiful wooden lodge with a fireplace and even a reading loft, unpacked, and followed the owner's ancient gunbearer out to a blind near a tree that he had baited for leopard. There was half a goat hanging down from a platform in the tree, and within twenty minutes a lovely female leopard appeared from nowhere, leaped up to the platform in a single bound, and began eating the goat. We stayed there, taking pictures until the light ran out, and finally returned to the lodge to hear more stories about the days when Kenya was still a frontier, men were men, and good cigars cost a nickel.

February 12: We left Maralal and drove about three hours to the Rift Valley, which in its entirety extends from Asian Russia to Botswana, but is nowhere more impressive than in East Africa. We stopped at Lake Baringo, hopped a boat, and went off to Island Camp, a tented camp at the southern tip of Baringo's largest island. (Also, I might add, its hilliest island; I don't recall any other portion of the trip, even the mountains, wearing me out as much as simply getting around Island Camp.)

When we reached our tent, I noticed a couple of lizards hanging on the walls and was all set to chase them away when Perry, who was in the next tent, explained that I would be very unhappy if I did so, since they took care of the insects, and that Lake Baringo, with its 100-degree temperatures, dense forests, and high humidity, had more than its share of insects. And, as Perry said, we went the entire day and night without so much as seeing an insect, let alone being bitten. (We were blessed with lizards the next six days, and when we finally came to a lodge that *didn't* have them—the luxurious Kilaguni Lodge in Tsavo National Park—I went right to the management and complained.) Baringo was a bird-watcher's paradise, and we spent most of the afternoon sitting in the open-air bar with our binoculars and cameras, watching everything from tiny weaver birds to fish eagles. The bar also contained, for reasons that were never properly explained to me, a semi-tame waterbuck that begged for beers and cleaned up most of the birdseed that was placed out for the weavers. Finally, in late afternoon, Perry and I borrowed a rather flimsy speedboat (Carol opted to remain behind, since she is a devout and dedicated bird-watcher), and went out searching for hippos and crocodiles. We found them, decided that our boat was even more delicate than it looked, and decided not to approach closer than about 40 yards, where we took a number of pictures and felt somewhat relieved that none of the hippos had been too curious about the boat.

February 13: We left Baringo and drove about 70 miles south to Lake Nakuru, home of some 2 million flamingos. I hopped out of the safari car and began carefully approaching them with my camera. They started backing away, I followed them, and after a few minutes I realized that something smelled *awful*. I finally took the camera away from my eye and found that I was surrounded for perhaps 50 yards in every direction by a 6-inch-deep patch of flamingo droppings. Still, I got the video footage I wanted—and a few hours later I got the bath I *needed*.

We spent only an hour or so at Nakuru, and then drove south another 50 miles to Lake Naivasha, the largest and prettiest of the Rift lakes. There's not all that much game at any of the lakes, but the birdlife is phenomenal, with up to 400 species at each of them. It was at Naivasha that I found an animal that rivaled Jumbo for my affections: he was a crested crane, and we named him Clyde. (He *looked* like a Clyde; if he could have worn a fur coat, gold jewelry, and lambchop sideburns, he would have.) Clyde lived on a lovely pond at our lodge, together with some Egyptian geese, a black swan, a white swan, and two lady crested cranes. Clyde was feeling the mating urge a little earlier than his ladyfriends were, and he spent most of the afternoon prancing and strutting his stuff for them. Anyway, there was a tortuously-twisted log spanning one segment of the pond, and at one point Clyde hopped onto the log, trilled a couple of times so that his ladies-in-waiting would look at him, and then began fluttering his wings and strutting like a professional wrestler for them—and slipped and fell head-first into the pond. He dragged himself to his feet, turned to make sure no one had seen him, and slipped again—and spent the better part of 40 seconds flopping around until he had finally regained his balance. Then, with more dignity than *I* could have mustered under the same circumstances, he shook himself off, gave us a look that said "I *meant* to do that!", and went right back to his fruitless courting of his ladyfriends. I loved him.

February 14: We drove a couple of hours to the Maasai Mara, which is actually the northern third of the Serengeti Plains. There wasn't much doubt of where we were when we arrived: less than a mile into the park we'd already seen a herd of more than 1,000 wildebeest, about 400 zebra, smaller herds of topi and hartebeest, a group of about 20 bachelor bull buffalo, and a herd of perhaps 40 elephants—and the further into the park we went, the more plentiful the game became. It was Hollywood's version of Africa: no matter where you stood, it was a safe bet that you were within 200 yards of at least 50 animals. My own guess is that we passed more than 5,000 Thomson's gazelle and 2,000 larger antelope on the way to our campsight. There was a time, and not so long ago at that, when all of East Africa looked like this; now only the Mara and Serengeti possess game in this quantity. The land was lush, green, dotted with thornbush and acacia trees, broken by narrow ribbons of water, and covered by more animals per square foot than anyone who hasn't been there can imagine. (Except rhinos. Poaching has lowered the Mara's rhino population from 5,500 in 1973 to 24 in

1985. There was one baby born this year, but lions got him.)

We stayed at Cottar's Camp, owned and run by a former white hunter named Glen Cottar. The manager was a young German named Mike Merten, who had discovered an American card game named "Oh Shit"—Carol and I knew it as "Oh Hell"—and who, once he discovered we had a deck of cards with us, insisted that we join him and his friends for a couple of hours of cards around the campfire every evening. It turned out that he had worked on *Sheena, Queen of the Jungle* and a couple of other films, and he, too, had a wealth of stories to share with us—as well as some money. (Sweet guy, lousy cardplayer.)

The accomodations were most interesting: papyrus structures with concrete floors, kind of a cross between a tent and a cabin, known as *bandas*. The camp, which is quite small, was filled with fascinating people. (The typical tourists stayed at the more famous and luxurious Keekorok Lodge, and the mavericks stayed here—and Perry figured, correctly, that a writer would find the mavericks more interesting.) One friend we made was Bryan, another card player, who was a gunsmith in Seattle and was making his leisurely way down to Zimbabwe to visit some relatives. He had planned to spend two days at Cottar's Camp and found the company so congenial that he had been there three weeks when we arrived. Bryan had been a Green Beret in Vietnam, and had been operating on a small mountain behind enemy lines when his group was spotted by a squad of Viet Cong. They killed all but one of the Cong, who ducked into a cave, and left Bryan behind to take care of him. Bryan decided that only a crazy man would go into a dark cave after an enemy who was hiding from him, and since he was an explosives expert, he tossed a pound of plastic explosive into the cave, walked about 200 feet away, and hit the detonator—and blew up the whole damned mountain. Evidently the cave was a major Viet Cong munitions dump—experts later estimated that, based on the explosion, it held 150 tons of rockets and other explosives—and when Bryan woke up, his buddies, assuming he was dead, were divvying up his possessions. He had dislocated every joint in his body, and spent the next couple of years in the hospital.

February 15: We got up even earlier than usual—usual was about 6:30 AM—and drove over to Keekorok to take a hot air balloon over the great herds of the Mara. We'd really been looking forward to this, but it was a bit disappointing. The basket was right under the butane pump which fueled the torch that heated the air, which meant that we got to wake up to the warming (read: *burning*) rays of butane on the back of our necks. Also, while the animals paid no attention to the balloon when it was silently drifting, they panicked every time the pilot hit the butane torch, which was every couple of minutes.

Anyway, the balloon stayed aloft about 90 minutes, and then started drifting over toward the Tanzania border, which was bad news since there are still border problems between the two countries. We soon passed the border, and suddenly the Sand River was coming up fast, and if we crossed *that* we were in big trouble, since the vans that were following us to take us back couldn't get across the river and we could expect a full day's hassle with the Tanzanian police—so our pilot decided to crash land. There were ten of us in the basket, and while no one was hurt it took us awhile to get untangled. On the other hand, we made some new acquaintences. The guy who had landed on top of me lives in Blue Ash, Ohio, not 5 miles from my house; while the little old lady who landed on Carol lives in Findlay, Ohio, where we've attended some science fiction conventions.

Once we got untangled, we were treated to an enormous champagne breakfast, and then drove back to Keekorok, during which time we realized just how much we appreciated both Perry and his car: the minibus' ride was terribly bumpy; Carol and I, having been trained by Perry, spotted all kinds of game that the driver missed; and when we came across a pride of lions on the move, we learned that minibus policy was to take a quick vote on whether to stop and photograph them or not, by which time they were gone anyway. As soon as we got back to Keekorok we hunted up Perry, who had wisely elected to take a nap rather than ride the balloon. If I point out a hill where we saw a herd of elephants from the balloon three hours ago, I said, do you think you can find them now? Silly question. Half an hour later we were right in the middle of them, snapping away, while the minibuses were searching fruitlessly for anything more exotic than gazelle and impala. We returned to camp for lunch (and the inevitable card game), then went out searching for lion—and found them. There was a large pride in the area of Cottar's Camp, ruled by a huge black-maned lion affectionately known as Number One. We never did find Number One, but we did find Numbers Two through Eighteen, inclusive. And returned for more beer, stories, and cards around the campfire.

February 16: Perry decided that we ought to see how the other half lives, so he arranged for us to visit the inside of a Maasai *manyatta*, an interesting if distasteful experience. The second I entered it (Carol, who is brighter than me, remained outside) I was totally covered by tsetse flies, just like the Maasai. The reason soon became apparent: they bring their cattle into the *manyatta* for safe-keeping every night, and what seemed like a dirt floor wasn't.

That done, we went out looking for Number One again. We still didn't find him, but we got some of the best photographs and footage we were to obtain on the safari. We came across a lioness nursing her cubs, and subtle, devious Perry got us to within ten yards of her without her ever knowing it. Then, perhaps a quarter of a mile away, we came to a lion "nursery": while most of the pride was out hunting, two lionesses had stayed behind with eleven cubs which were from five or six different litters. Again, we managed to get to within about ten yards of the closest of them, and spent a couple of hours watching and photographing them as they played and frolicked.

Perry left at noon to make the long drive over poor roads to Nairobi, and we remained behind to play more cards, swap more stories, drink more Tuskers, and go on a final game run with a local game ranger Perry had asked to look after us. We saw still more lions and elephant and buffalo and giraffe and antelope, and we still couldn't find Number One. Win a few, lose a few.

February 17: We got up at dawn, couldn't escape yet another card game, and had Mike Merten drive us to the local airstrip a couple of miles away at 9:00. Where is it, I asked as we stopped on a green plain in front of some 200 zebra. You're looking at it, he answered, and about two minutes later a small 5-seater came into view, buzzed the zebra until they dispersed, and then landed and taxied right up to the car. We climbed aboard and the pilot took off and flew us to Governor's Camp, on the far side of the Mara, which had a tarmac landing strip that could accomodate a plane large enough to fly to Nairobi.

It was a few minutes late—elephants on the landing strip—but eventually it landed, and about 30 of us, who had been flown there from all over the Mara, climbed aboard. The stewardess handed out little mimeographed sheets giving the history of the plane: it was a DC-3 that had been commissioned in 1944, had seen action in the Berlin airlift, and had never missed a single day of service. None of which made me feel any better as it reached its cruising altitude of only 8,500 feet and let the wind play games with it all the way to Nairobi, where, according to Perry (who was there waiting for us) it bounced about 20 feet into the air after first touching the ground before it finally decided to land.

We ate lunch at the Carnivore, where we met yet another of Perry's friends with stories to tell, and then drove down to Amboseli, perhaps the most famous and surely the most frequently-visited of all Kenya's parks. We knew pretty much what to expect, but the reality was even more depressing than we had anticipated. Amboseli is a park that is, quite simply, used up. Not all parks have to be as lush and green as the Mara; Buffalo Springs, for example, was absolutely beautiful in its starkness. But Amboseli is nothing more than a dust bowl. According to Perry, it was *always* a dust bowl...but it has become even worse since the elephants began destroying their environment. Amboseli is home to about 1,200 elephants, which is about 800 more than it should hold. They have destroyed almost all the trees, most of the bushes and shrubs, and half the grass. We saw zebras literally choking on the dust they raised as they walked from one meagre clump of grass to another. There's water, and there's game, but Amboseli nevertheless gives the impression of a doomed ecosystem that's simply running down.

February 18: We awoke before dawn, since Mt. Kilimanjaro was covered by clouds when we arrived and Perry felt that dawn was the one sure time we'd be able to see and photograph it. He was right, as always. And, since we were up, we decided to take our game run before breakfast in the hope of getting out ahead of the other tourists and avoiding some of the dust their cars and buses raised. Unfortunately, most of them had the same idea, and the dust rising from the dirt roads was almost impenetrable in places. We spent two hours looking for rhino (whose number in Kenya have diminished from 20,000 to a mere 500 since 1973), but there were none to be found—at least, not in the area we covered. We did see quite a few elephant, some hippo, and a couple of thousand wildebeest. However, once it became apparent we weren't going to turn up any rhino, we decided to eat and hit the road, since we had no desire to spend any more time in Amboseli.

We drove to Tsavo West, and checked into the luxurious Kilaguni Lodge, where we once again ran into Tessa Gross, the girl who had trained horses for *Out of Africa*. She joined us for a game run and a trip to Mzima Springs, where some 97 million gallons a day of cold, fresh water flow down from Kilimanjaro. The springs, which supply distant Mombasa with all of its fresh water, are home to hundreds of hippos and crocs, and we got some lovely footage there.

Then we returned to Kilaguni for dinner. While we were eating (in the usual open-air restaurant overlooking the usual waterhole) an old elephant lumbered out of the hills and came down to slake his thirst just after dusk. Next came a pair of cow elephants and their babies. Then four more cows and three babies. Then half a dozen bachelor males. Then some teenagers. They kept coming, and by 9:00 PM there must have been more than 200 elephants quietly drinking, grazing and socializing (that's not an anthropomorphism; elephants *do* socialize). It was too dark to photograph them, but since it was our last night on the veldt we were reluctant to go to bed, and so we sat out on our balcony, simply watching them. Just after midnight they began dispersing in utter silence, heading off into the hills in twos and threes and fours. By one o'clock the last of them was gone, and there was not a single sign that they had ever been there at all. It was a memorable and moving experience which we will carry with us forever.

February 19: We drove to Mombasa, which was about a zillion degrees and a billion percent humidity (in the shade; it was warmer in the sunlight). The drive was so long and hot that when we got to our room at the newly-opened Inter-Continental Hotel (the first air-conditioned quarters we'd experienced in Africa, and the first telephone we'd seen since the Norfolk), we decided to spend the rest of the day unwinding. We did a little gift-shopping in the afternoon, had a lovely dinner at their outdoor restaurant on the beach (it was also our first look at the Indian Ocean), stuck around for the entertainment (an imported singer from England), left a little money in their casino, and slept in a delightful penthouse suite that, for a change, didn't require lizards.

February 20: We got up very early, while the temperature was still below 90, and drove into Mombasa, which has to be the most exotic city I've ever seen. It's about 50% black, 20% Indian, 15% Arab, 5% Oriental, and 10% white. The streets wind and twist back upon themselves, the odors are guaranteed to wake such dead as aren't otherwise occupied at the time, most of the buildings are at least a century old (and some were built prior to 1600), and you truly expect to bump into Sydney Greenstreet or Peter Lorre around the next corner. I had some research to do for *Ivory*, the novel I'll be working on this autumn, and Perry dutifully led us to all the sites I had to visit. We managed to wrap it up in about three hours and got back to the hotel before the thermometer topped 110 degrees.

Carol, who was finally back in good health, decided not to jeopardize it by going out again, but I wanted to go to a couple of gift shops—there was a particular book I was looking for—so Perry and I went back out after lunch to check out the gift shops at some nearby hotels. It proved fruitless: they may well have had the book, but since I don't read German there was no way to tell. (In fact, a tour of the local hotels could lead one to conclude that the Third Reich won the war. So overwhelmingly German were the patrons that all the books, signs, menus, everything, were printed only in German.)

We decided that as long as we were out, we might as well drive around a little, and before long we came to a tiny sign pointing the way to the Jumba National Monument. I asked Perry what it was, and he confessed that he had never heard of it, so we decided to follow the sign's directions. We went down an incredibly bumpy dirt road for three miles, past a chicken farm and a couple of flower nurseries, and finally came to a little cottage. We got out, paid a tiny admission fee (something like seven cents apiece), followed a narrow path—and came to a truly remarkable set of ruins of an Arab village, Jumba La Mtwana ("House of the Male Slaves"), which dated back to 1350 A.D. There were about 20 buildings, including a couple of large mosques. Many of the walls were intact, and while ruins usually bore me to tears, I found these fascinating.

We spent a couple of hours there, then returned to the hotel. All during dinner I kept telling Carol about the ruins, and all during the buffet dinner we kept fighting off the French guests, who were indulging in a typical French feeding frenzy, and by desert we had the plot for a science fiction novel. It is tentatively titled *Remains*, and the voracious French tourists were every bit as important to it as the Arab ruins. If any of those luxury beach resorts had been frequented by the English or the Americans, I'd have found the book I was looking for, we'd have skipped visiting the ruins, and I'd have come home with material for one less novel.

February 21: We left early to beat the heat, and drove the 300 miles back to Nairobi. And, since we left at dawn and I had been up past midnight the past three nights, I fell asleep in the car—with my left arm hanging out the window the whole way. I'd been in Africa for more than two weeks and had gotten a Stewart Granger suntan; now, on my last full day there, I managed to get a 2nd-degree sunburn on my arm.

We checked in at the Norfolk again, went into town to do a little shopping, took another trip to Karen Blixen's house (we hadn't had our cameras the first time and wanted some pictures), and ate dinner in the famed

Ibis Grill, from which Lord Delamere used to pot elephants whenever he was drunk, which was almost every night.

February 22: We ate breakfast in the Delamere Lounge (from which a drunken Lord Delamore used to shoot elephants when he wasn't doing it down the hall in the Ibis Grill), drove to the airport, and caught the plane to London—via Cyprus. I was at a loss to understand this, since the flight *to* Nairobi was nonstop, no one was getting on or off at Cyprus, and Cyprus isn't exactly the safest place to be these days, especially if you're disguised as an American. The co-pilot finally explained it to me: when we took off from London, we were taking off at sea level, at which point the engines were working at 100% efficiency, and could lift the plane off the ground carrying all the fuel it required to reach Nairobi. But Nairobi is at an altitude of 6,000 feet, and the engines couldn't lift the fully-fueled plane at that altitude. So we landed in Cyprus and were immediately surrounded by half a dozen tanks and about 500 armed soldiers, who refused to allow the plane to go anywhere near the terminal. We sat there for a couple of hours while their military decided whether or not to give us the fuel we needed. (It happens every day, and they give the airplane the necessary fuel every day, but they always take their time about it, which gives the passengers a final adventure to relate when they arrive home.)

February 23: There's not a hell of a lot to do in London on a Sunday, so we met my daughter, Laura, at the British Museum and spent the afternoon there. Makes one admire the industry of the Brits, while questioning their morals: if something wasn't nailed down—a mummy, a small temple, *anything*—they plundered it and shipped it back to England. I am convinced the only reason there are no pyramids in the museum is because they couldn't figure out how to send one home.

February 24: Visited my British agent and a couple of editors, spent the rest of the day with Carol and Laura shopping for books that are unavailable in the States, and went off to see the highly-lauded musical, *Les Miserables*. We see perhaps 12 to 15 plays a year in New York and England, and candidly, this was the most boring piece of theater we've attended in well over a decade.

February 25: Landed in New York after a 7-hour trip, and gave Barry Malzberg a call while we were waiting for the flight to Cincinnati. He told me of the shocking number of deaths that had occurred within the science fiction community while we were gone—L. Ron Hubbard, Frank Herbert, Judy-Lynn del Rey—which forcefully brought home the fact that there are a lot more dangerous things to do than sneak up on lions and elephants, like just trying to keep your machinery running. We got home at about 10:00 PM, said hello to our various and sundry animals, and fell to work opening a 5-foot-high stack of mail. The very first letter was from Eleanor Wood, informing me that *Santiago* had made the B. Dalton and Waldenbooks bestseller lists in its first week of release. It almost—but not quite—made me glad to be back.

STALKING THE UNICORN WITH GUN AND CAMERA

I had always wanted to write a parody of a how-to hunting article for hairy-chested he-men. It was when I saw one too many paintings of innocent, soft-eyed unicorns at a science fiction convention's art show that I realized that I had finally come across the perfect subject matter.

When she got to within 200 yards of the herd of Southern Savannah unicorns she had been tracking for four days, Rheela of the Seven Stars made her obeisance to Quatr Mane, God of the Hunt, then donned the Amulet of Kobassen, tested the breeze to make sure that she was still downwind of the herd, and began approaching them, camera in hand.

But Rheela of the Seven Stars had made one mistake—a mistake of *carelessness*—and thirty seconds later she was dead, brutally impaled upon the horn of a bull unicorn.

Hotack the Beastslayer cautiously made his way up the lower slopes of the Mountain of the Nameless One. He was a skilled tracker, a fearless hunter, and a crack shot. He picked out the trophy he wanted, got the beast within his sights, and hurled his killing club. It flew straight and true to its mark.

And yet, less than a minute later, Hotack, his left leg badly gored, was barely able to pull himself to safety in the branches of a nearby Rainbow Tree. He, too, had make a mistake—a mistake of *ignorance*.

Bort the Pure had had a successful safari. He had taken three chimeras, a gorgon, and a beautifully-matched pair of griffons. While his trolls were skinning the gorgon he spotted a unicorn sporting a near-record horn, and, weapon in hand, he began pursuing it. The terrain gradually changed, and suddenly Bort found himself in shoulder-high Kraken grass. Undaunted, he followed the trail into the dense vegetation.

But Bort the Pure, too, had made a mistake—a mistake of *foolishness*. His trolls found what very little remained of him some six hours later.

Carelessness, ignorance, foolishness—together they account for more deaths among unicorn hunters than all other factors combined.

Take our examples, for instance. All three hunters—Rheela, Hotack, and Bort—were experienced safari hands. They were used to extremes of temperature and terrain, they didn't object to finding insects in their ale or banshees in their tents, they knew they were going after deadly game and took all reasonable precautions before setting out.

And yet two of them died, and the third was badly maimed. Let's examine their mistakes, and see what we can learn from them:

Rheela of the Seven Stars assimilated everything her personal wizard could tell her about unicorns, purchased the very finest photographic equipment, hired a native guide who had been on many unicorn hunts, and had a local witch doctor bless her Amulet of Kobassen. And yet, when the charge came, the amulet was of no use to her, for she had failed to properly identify the particular sub-species of unicorn before her—and as I am continually pointing out during my lecture tours, the Amulet of Kobassen is potent only against the rare and almost-extinct Forest unicorn. Against the Southern Savannah unicorn, the *only* effective charm is the Talisman of Triconis. *Carelessness.*

Hotack the Beastslayer, on the other hand, disdained all forms of supernatural protection. To him, the essence of the hunt was to pit himself in physical combat against his chosen prey. His killing club, a beautifully-wrought and finely-balanced instrument of destruction, had brought down simurghs, humbabas, and even a dreaded wooly hydra. He elected to go for a head shot, and the club flew to within a milimeter of where he had aimed it. But he hadn't counted on the unicorn's phenomenal sense of smell, nor the speed with which these surly brutes can move. Alerted to Hotack's presence, the unicorn turned its head to seek out its predator—and the killing club bounced harmlessly off its horn. Had Hotack spoken to almost any old-time unicorn hunter, he would have realized that head shots are almost impossible, and would have gone for a crippling knee shot. *Ignorance.*

Bort the Pure was aware of the unique advantages accruing to a virgin who hunts the wild unicorn, and so had practiced sexual abstinence since he was old enough to know what the term meant. And yet he naively believed that because his virginity allowed him to approach the unicorn more easily than other hunters, the unicorn would somehow become placid and make no attempt to defend itself—and so he followed a vicious animal which was compelled to let him approach it, and entered a patch of high grass which allowed him no maneuvering room during the inevitable charge. *Foolishness.*

Every year hundreds of hopeful hunters go out in search of the unicorn, and every year all but a handful come back empty-handed—if they come back at all. And yet the unicorn *can* be safely stalked and successfully hunted, if only the stalkers and hunters will take the time to study their quarry.

When all is said and done, the unicorn is a relatively docile beast (except when enraged). It is a creature of habit, and once those habits have been learned by the hopeful photographer or trophy hunter, bringing home that picture or that horn is really no more dangerous than, say, slaying an Eight-Forked Dragon—and it's certainly easier than lassoing wild minotaurs, a sport that has become all the rage these days among the smart set on the Platinum Plains.

However, before you can photograph or kill a unicorn, you have to find it—and by far the easiest way to make contact with a unicorn herd is to follow the families of smerps that track the great game migrations. The smerps, of course, have no natural enemies except for the rafsheen and the zumakim, and consequently will allow a human (or preternatural) being to approach them quite closely.

A word of warning about the smerp: with its long ears and cute, fuzzy body, it resembles nothing more than an oversized rabbit—but calling a smerp a rabbit doesn't make it one, and you would be ill-advised to underestimate the strength of these nasty little scavengers. Although they generally hunt in packs of from ten to twenty, I have more than once seen a single smerp, its aura glowing with savage strength, pull down a half-grown unicorn. Smerps are poor eating, their pelts are worthless because of the difficulty of curing and tanning the auras, and they make pretty unimpressive trophies unless you can come up with one possessing a truly magnificent set of ears—in fact, in many areas they're still classified as vermin—but the wise unicorn hunter can save himself a lot of time and effort by simply letting the smerps lead him to his prey.

With the onset of poaching, the legendary unicorn herds numbering upwards of a thousand members no longer exist, and you'll find that the typical herd today consists of from 50 to 75 individuals. The days when a photographer, safe and secure in a blind by a waterhole, could preserve on film an endless stream of the brutes coming down to drink, are gone forever—and it is absolutely shocking to contemplate the number of unicorns that have died simply so their horns could be sold on the black market. In fact, I find it appalling that anyone in this enlightened day and age still believes that a powdered unicorn horn can act as an aphrodisiac.

(Indeed, as any magi can tell you, you treat the unicorn horn with essence of *gracch* and then boil it slowly in a solution of sphinx blood. Now *that's* an aphrodisiac!)

But I digress.

The unicorn, being a non-discriminating browser that is equally content to feed upon grasses, leaves, fruits, and an occasional small fern tree, occurs in a wide variety of habitats, often in the company of grazers such as centaurs and ~~pegasuses pegasim~~ the pegasus.

Once you have spotted the unicorn herd, it must be approached with great care and caution. The unicorn may have poor eyesight, and its sense of hearing may not be much better, but it has an excellent sense of smell and an absolutely awesome sense of *grimsch*, about which so much has been written that there is no point in my belaboring the subject yet again.

If you are on a camera safari, I would strongly advise against trying to get closer than 100 yards to even a solitary beast—that sense of *grimsch* again—and most of the photographers I know swear by an 85-350mm automatic-focus zoom lens, providing, of course, that it has been blessed by a Warlock of the Third Order. If you haven't got the shots you want by sunset, my best advice is to pack it in for the day and return the next morning. Flash photography is possible, of course, but it does tend to attract golem and other even more bothersome nocturnal predators.

One final note to the camera buff: For reasons our alchemists have not yet determined, no unicorn has ever been photographed with normal emulsified film of any speed, so make absolutely sure that you use one of the more popular infrared brands. It would be a shame to spend weeks on safari, paying for your guide, cook, and trolls, only to come away with a series of photos of the forest that you thought was merely the background to your pictures.

As for hunting the brutes, the main thing to remember is that they are as close to you as you are to them. For this reason, while I don't disdain blood sacrifices, amulets, talismans, and blessings, all of which have their proper place, I for one always feel more confident with a .550 Nitro Express in my hands. A little extra stopping power can give a hunter quite a feeling of security.

You'll want a bull unicorn, of course; they tend to have more spectacular horns than the cows—and by the time a bull's horn is long enough to be worth taking, he's probably too old to be in the herd's breeding program anyway.

The head shot, for reasons explained earlier, is never a wise option. And unless your wizard teaches you the Rune of Mamhotet, thus enabling you the approach close enough to pour salt on the beast's tail and thereby pin him to the spot where he's standing, I recommend the heart shot (either heart will do—and if you have a double-barreled gun, you might try to hit both of them, just to be on the safe side.)

If you have the bad fortune to merely wound the beast, he'll immediately make off for the trees or the high grass, which puts you at an enormous disadvantage. Some hunters, faced with such a situation, merely stand back and allow the smerps to finish the job for them—after all, smerps rarely devour the horn unless they're completely famished—but this is hardly sporting. The decent, honorable hunter, well aware of the unwritten rules of blood sports, will go after the unicorn himself.

The trick, of course, is to meet him on fairly open terrain. Once the unicorn lowers his head to charge, he's virtually blind, and all you need do is dance nimbly out of his way and take another shot at him—or, if you are not in possession of the Rune of Mamhotet, this would be an ideal time to get out that salt and try to sprinkle some on his tail as he races by.

When the unicorn dictates the rules of the game, you've got a much more serious situation. He'll usually double back and lie in the tall grasses beside his spoor, waiting for you to pass by, and then attempt to gore you from behind.

It is at this time that the hunter must have all his wits about him. Probably the best sign to look for is the presence of Fire-Breathing Dragonflies. These noxious little insects frequently live in symbiosis with the unicorn, cleansing his ears of parasites, and their presence usually means that the unicorn isn't far off. Yet another sign that your prey is nearby will be the flocks of hungry harpies circling overhead, waiting to swoop down and feed upon the remains of your kill; and, of course, the surest sign of all is when you hear a grunt of rage and find yourself staring into the bloodshot, beady little eyes of a wounded bull unicorn from a distance of ten feet or less. It's moments like that that make you feel truly alive, especially when you suddenly realize that it isn't necessarily a permanent condition.

All right. Let us assume that your hunt is successful. What then?

Well, your trolls will skin the beast, of course, and take special care in removing and preserving the horn. If they've been properly trained they'll also turn the pelt into a rug, the hooves into ashtrays, the teeth into a necklace, the tail into a flyswatter, and the scrotum into a tobacco pouch. My own feeling is that you should settle for nothing less, since it goes a long way toward showing the bleeding-heart preservationists that a unicorn can supply the hunter with a lot more than just a few minutes of pleasurable sport and a horn.

And while I'm on the subject of what the unicorn can supply, let me strongly suggest that you would be missing a truly memorable experience if you were to come home from safari without having eaten unicorn meat at least once. There's nothing quite like unicorn cooked over an open campfire to top off a successful hunt. (And do remember to leave something out for the smerps, or they might well decide that hunter is every bit as tasty as unicorn.)

So get out those amulets and talismans, visit those wizards and warlocks, pack those cameras and weapons—and good hunting to you!

Next Week: *Outstaring the Medusa*

JUMBO

When I described the subject matter of
Ivory *to Shereen Karmali, the editor of*
Swara, *the official publication of the East*
African Wildlife Society, she asked me if
I'd write an article about the research that
went into the novel. I was happy to oblige.

He was the greatest animal to stride the Earth
since the dawn of human history, and yet almost
nothing is known of him.

The place of his birth is unrecorded. There are no
verifiable eyewitness accounts of him. Even the time
and circumstances of his death are shrouded in mystery.

And yet there is no doubt that he existed. What
remains of him can be viewed, by appointment, in the
basement of the British Museum of Natural History.

He is known only as the Kilimanjaro Elephant, and
his tusks are the largest on record. At the time of his
death one weighed 237.5 pounds and the other 225; even
today, after they've had almost a century to lose
moisture content, the larger still weighs considerably
over 220 pounds, and the smaller easily tops 210. Pick
up a copy of Rowland Ward's *African Records of Big*
Game and you'll find that most game records are
separated by a fraction of an inch, a portion of a pound.
Not the Kilimanjaro Elephant. No other tusk has ever
weighed as much as 200 pounds. This animal was, in
terms of physical proportion, a monster; even the famed
Ahmed of Marsabit would look small next to him.

But it was the total mystery concerning him, even more than his gargantuan dimensions, that piqued my interest in him. I am a novelist by profession, and after coming across a sufficient number of references to him (or, more specifically, to his ivory) in my readings on Africa—Bell, Blunt, Smith, Lyell, and perhaps a dozen others all have their own versions, none of them first-hand accounts, most of them contradictory—it occurred to me that there might be a story to be told.

I had been long overdue to take a safari in Kenya anyway, so I decided to kill two birds with one stone by following the trail of the Kilimanjaro Elephant (hereinafter to be known, less formally, as Jumbo) at a considerable distance—not of yards or miles, but of years: 88 of them, to be precise. To help me in this endeavor I acquired the services of Perry Mason, who runs an excellent safari company operating out of Nairobi.

The first problem was where to start. Donald Ker had mentioned a legendary tusker named Mai in his memoirs, but the years were all wrong: Jumbo's ivory was sold at auction in 1898, and Ker had actually seen Mai in 1932. There were references in other books to a huge elephant named Selimundi, whose tusks plowed up furrows of earth as he walked, but he was seen thousands of miles away from Kilimanjaro, and when we plotted out his likely range we were able to eliminate him.

So we started from scratch. Where were the biggest tusks usually found? Perry suggested that it would very likely be north of the Tana River. Marsabit? At least, that's where all the big tuskers were now. Perhaps—but I ruled it out. Most Marsabit elephants tend to remain at Marsabit; why walk through 200 miles of desert when there's year-around food and water in your back yard? The input and expertise were Perry's, but the decisions were all mine, and I decided that it was more likely that he came from considerably further south, so, after unwinding from our flight in the Aberdares and Mount

Kenya for a couple of days, we made the Buffalo Springs/Samburu area our first official port of call. There was, of course, no way to verify that Jumbo had ever been there, but it *felt* right, and fiction writers tend go with their gut instincts—especially when there's no contradictory source material.

All right. To get that kind of ivory growth, Jumbo had to be an old elephant when he died: 55 at least, possibly as old as 70. I split the difference and put his age, at the time of his death, at 62.

He was smart, too; he had to be, to stay alive with a couple of world-record trophies protruding from his mouth. Now we began to work backward. If he died on the northeastern slopes of Kilimanjaro, how large was his range and how long did it take him to get from the Northern Frontier District to the mountain? Logic dictated that, given his age and experience, his knowledge of the seasons and his having gone through droughts, he wouldn't have waited for the dry season to begin migrating south. It made sense that he would have started after the long rains, where he could find water along the way, perhaps in July.

There were a lot of routes to the south. Which way would he have gone?

The coast was settled, but Kenya's interior was still pretty much as it had always been. The railroad wasn't completed yet, and Nairobi was little more than an outpost. Surely he'd avoid such civilization as existed (remember: there are no eyewitness descriptions of him, and he was certainly an elephant people would have remembered), but as I studied the map, it struck me that if he was moving during the dry season, he'd have the easiest time of it in the Rift Valley, where the lakes provided ample water and where European settlers hadn't yet made any great inroads.

So the Rift lakes were next on my agenda, after breaking the trip for a day at Maralal. We hit Bogoria, Baringo, Nakuru and Naivasha, taking photos and notes and trying to trace his hopefully-not-mythical journey.

Would he have then gone southwest to the Mara? Not very likely, so Jumbo's trek was put on the back burner for a few days while Perry took my wife and I to the Mara for the non-working part of the safari.

Then it was over to Amboseli. If indeed he came from north of the Tana, he *must* have passed through here to get to the mountain. How long did he spend on his way from Naivasha? Did he temporarily join a herd and make some little Jumbos? Were there side-trips?

There's no way to know, though the book will make some guesses. Then he began ascending Kilimanjaro—and there he died.

Karamojo Bell claims to have been told by a slave trader named Shundi that Jumbo was shot by one of Shundi's own slaves—but while there is no reason to disbelieve Bell, there is every reason to disbelieve Shundi, who sent the tusks on to Zanzibar to be sold. Why would he have lied? Well, for one reason, he was already wanted for slave-trading, and probably had no desire to add ivory poaching (or ivory stealing) to the list. For another, he would hardly have impressed Bell with his *macho* competence if he had admitted that he simply stumbled across the corpse of a giant elephant that had either died of old age or slipped and fallen to its death. I don't say that either of my versions are true, but only that when I read Bell's account they seemed as likely as the story Shundi told him. (Later, after examining Jumbo's tusks, I revised my opinion: Shundi may have chanced upon the corpse or stolen the ivory from whoever obtained it first, but he definitely didn't poach it.)

A trip to Zanzibar was out of the question; we had no visas, and after a couple of days of relaxing in Tsavo we were running out of time—writers may not have regular hours, but they *do* have deadlines—so I decided to make do with Mombasa. We hunted up the old ivory market, the one that had been in business in 1898, just to get the feel of the place, spent a day on the beach and another shopping in Nairobi, bid Perry Mason farewell, and began the trip home, via the British Museum of Natural History. Jumbo's tusks are in the care of Dr. Juliet Jewell. I had written ahead to get permission to examine them, and she very graciously allowed me all the time I needed with them. The most obvious conclusion to be reached is that, however he died, Jumbo wasn't killed for his ivory. They had been hacked out sloppily and unevenly, and no poacher or trophy hunter would have wasted that much ivory.

Which leads to one of two conclusions: first, that Jumbo was killed in self-defense, and that the ivory was removed as an afterthought; or second, that he died of natural causes, and that the ivory was chopped out within a very few days (since decomposition would have allowed whoever discovered him to pull it out very neatly if he'd been dead any length of time).

And so I returned home, having tracked Jumbo through his final journey as best I could, and began making notes. My notion was to begin with his last year of life, and then to follow the ivory through a totally fictional journey, chronicling all the lives it touched and changed, until it wound up in the British Museum of Natural History.

I submitted an outline to my agent, entitling the novel *Ivory*, and waited for her to shower me with praise. What I received instead was a challenge.

She pointed out that my fame, such as it is, is as a science fiction writer. That's where my audience is, and that's where my sales are. She might be able to sell the book as conceived, of course—but if I would be willing to follow the ivory for the next few thousand years, possibly even into space...

I got the picture—and, after expanding the scope of the outline, I got the contract. And now, instead of writing *Ivory* while what I saw is still fresh in my mind, I'll be spending the next few months constructing the future as I had reconstructed the past.

On the other hand, I'll get to right a great wrong. I don't know the whole of their journey yet, but eventually Jumbo's tusks are going to return to Mount Kilimanjaro's fertile soil, to join the rest of his remains.

After getting a fascinating safari and a lucrative book contract from the fabled Kilimanjaro Elephant, I owe him that much.

The Hunter

*Ivory, nominated at this writing for a Best
Novel Nebula for 1989 and probably my
most successful novel to date, was inspired
by an animal known as the Kilimanjaro
Elephant, and chronicles an
eight-millennia quest for his tusks. This
excerpt—chronologically the earliest—is
set in 1885 A.D., and tells the story of the
only white man ever to see him during his
lifetime.*

Old Van der Kamp looked around the barroom at
the dusty shack he called the Mbogo Trading Post and
totaled up the white faces: three—four, if he counted
himself—which was more than he could ever remember
being there at the same time.

Named for the buffalo that had given him a game
leg before he'd finally managed to put a bullet through
its eye, the trading post had been sitting there on the
Sand River, gathering customers and termites in equal
proportions, for the better part of two decades. In the
back room the old Boer kept piles upon piles of skins
and ivory, each carefully labeled as to supplier and
amount paid, against the day that the rains would come
again and the riverboat could come by and pick them
up. In an adjacent cellar, buried deep in the earth to
help keep them cool, were some 20 kegs of beer. Van der
Kamp offered no menu and no food, but if a passing

traveler brought enough for everyone, he had no objection to cooking it up.

Hanging on the wall behind the bar were the gleaming white skulls and horns—Van der Kamp could not afford a taxidermist—of kudu, sable, roan, eland, a clutch of gazelles, and the buffalo that had given the outpost its name.

The old man drew himself another beer and observed his clientele. Sitting at one end of the bar in neatly-pressed clothes was the Englishman, Rice, his carefully-trimmed goatee almost pure white, his hands strong and calloused, most of the color washed out of his face from too much exposure to the tropical sun. It was odd, reflected Van der Kamp, but instead of getting darker, the English seemed to lose such color as they had acquired after a few years and wound up paler than when they had come out.

At the opposite end of the bar was Guntermann, the German: bald, moustached, with blue eyes and a suit that had once been white but was now the color of the scorched African earth. Even here inside the shack he wore his pith helmet, more to hide his bald head from view than to protect it from the sun. Still, as strange as he looked, he knew his business; 42 tusks bearing his name now resided in the storage room.

Sitting quietly at the lone table at the back of the room was Sloane, the first American Van der Kamp had ever seen. Americans were rare in Africa, since their government had no colonial ambitions anywhere on the continent. This one certainly looked out of place, with his cowboy stetson and his Confederate Army uniform, but he had already made a name for himself as an ivory hunter, leading the old Boer to conclude that if there was one thing that the men who stopped at the Mbogo Trading Post had in common, it was that they had nothing in common.

Outside the building, sitting in a sheltered area near the bore hole, were some twenty blacks, bearers and trackers for the three white men. They weren't allowed inside, but Van der Kamp saw to it that they got all the beer they wanted, a foul-smelling Kisi brew that packed quite a punch and for which he charged their employers what he thought was a nominal fee. He had checked them out carefully: a Lumbwa, a Kikuyu, nine Wakamba, half a dozen Nandi, a Wanderobo, and a pair of Bugandas. No Maasai, praise be, which meant that there probably wouldn't be any blood-letting. He stuck his head out the window every few minutes, keeping a watchful eye on the big, well-muscled Lumbwa, just to be on the safe side, but the Lumbwa, sitting off by himself, seemed oblivious to the presence of the other Africans.

"I'll have another," announced Rice as he drained his glass. He looked around the room for a moment. "My treat, if anyone should care to join me."

Sloane, the American, looked up, nodded his agreement, and went back to rolling a cigarette.

"I would be delighted," said the German, taking out a handkerchief and wiping the sweat from his face. "Allow me to introduce myself: I am Erhard Guntermann, late of Munich."

"Guntermann, Guntermann," mused Rice. Suddenly he looked across at the German. "Didn't I hear your name in connection with a slave-running operation some years back?"

"I hope not," said the German with a hearty laugh. "I have done my best to disassociate myself with that particular part of my past." He shrugged. "There wasn't much money in it anyway," he added with a sly smile. "Too much competition from the English." He paused. "Besides, ivory pays much better."

"Gentlemen, the Queen," said Rice, holding his glass up. Nobody followed suit, which didn't seem to bother him at all. "So you're an ivory hunter now?"

Guntermann shook his head. "I'm an ivory *trader*."

"Oh?

The German nodded. "I go to the Congo, into the rain forest, and when I find tribes that are starved for meat, I supply antelope to them in exchange for ivory." He paused and wiped his face again. "Very profitable," he added with satisfaction.

"But if they can kill elephants, why can't they kill their own meat?" asked Rice, slapping at a tsetse fly that had landed on his neck.

"They don't kill many elephants themselves," explained the German. "But they know where to find the carcasses, and when they find them, they collect the ivory." He paused long enough for a series of hippo grunts from the nearby river to subside. "One pygmy village had so much ivory they used it for fenceposts around their *bomas*!" The German shook his head in mock sorrow. "Poor people. They have no idea what it's worth."

"Where was this village with ivory fenceposts?" asked Rice curiously.

Guntermann smiled. "Ah, my friend, you do not really expect me to tell you that, do you?"

Rice returned his smile. "No, not really." He continued staring at the German as the bellowing of the hippos began again. "So you're Guntermann."

"That's me," said Guntermann. "And you?"

"Blaney Rice, formerly of Johannesburg."

"Johannesburg," repeated the German. "You were born in Africa?"

"I was born in Manchester, England. I emigrated to South Africa and started a farm there, and when it went broke, I began trading my way north." He paused. "I ended up here twelve years later. That was, oh, about ten years ago."

"You trade ivory?" asked Guntermann with professional interest.

"Not any longer," replied Rice, picking up a nut from a bowl on the bar and tossing it to a vervet monkey that appeared in the window. The monkey screeched and ducked, then picked it up off the ground and reappeared in the window a moment later, looking for another tidbit.

"What *do* you trade?"

Rice smiled. "Photographs."

"Photographs?" repeated the German disbelievingly.

Rice nodded. "I use architects' blueprint paper," he explained. "I trade the photos to the village headmen for salt, trade the salt for copper, the copper for goats, the goats for more salt, and the salt for cattle. It takes half a year to make my circuit and get to the Sudan, where I sell the cattle to the army—but when I'm finished, I've usually made about three thousand pounds on an initial investment of six shillings."

"Before you sold photographs, what?" asked the German, plucking a small insect from his handkerchief, studying it idly, and flicking it to the floor.

"I started out to make my fortune as an ivory hunter," replied Rice, "but I must confess I wasn't very good at it. When I quit, I hadn't so much as a halfpenny to my name, and I discovered that the only thing I had that was worth anything at all to the locals were my cartridges. I traded them for salt, sold the salt for more cartridges, traded them for goats, and kept on going until I reached Abyssinia and sold out for almost two thousand Maria Theresa dollars. It was too hot up there, so I came down here where the weather was more pleasant and there were more tribes to trade with, bought a couple of cameras, and went into business."

"You call *this* pleasant weather?" asked Sloane sardonically.

Rice turned to him. "Have you ever been up in Abyssinia?"

"A couple of times."

"Then you know how hot it gets there."

"Not a hell of a lot hotter than right here," said Sloane.

"You're quite wrong," said Rice adamantly. "No man was meant to live in that heat."

Sloane shrugged and turned his attention back to his beer.

"I have a question for you, my good sir, if you don't mind?" continued Rice.

Sloane stared at him for a moment. "Go ahead," he said at last.

"The native you arrived with," said Rice. "I don't seem to recognize his tribal markings."

"He's a Kikuyu."

"I've never seen one before," said Rice. "I had heard that Kikuyuland was closed to whites."

"It is."

"Then how did you acquire him?"

"He broke a law, and escaped before they could kill him," said Sloane.

"What did he do?"

Sloane shrugged. "I never asked him."

"Are the Kikuyus good trackers?" asked Rice.

"This one's all right," said Sloane noncommittally.

"Not like the Wanderobo, though," said Guntermann with a touch of pride as a change of breeze brought the unmistakable odors of hippopotamus and crocodile to them on the hot, moist air.

"I noticed that you had one with you," commented Rice, fanning himself with his hat, more to chase the smells of the river away than from any serious belief that the effort might make him feel cooler. "Are they as good as people say?"

"My Wanderobo could track a billiard ball down the smoothest street in Berlin," responded Guntermann.

Rice chuckled and finished his beer, then held up his empty glass. "I believe it's someone else's turn?"

"Acknowledged," said Guntermann, slapping down a few coins. "Now that you have brought up the subject of Wanderobo, I saw a Wanderobo woman behind the building when I arrived."

"She is Kisi," answered Van der Kamp. He paused, then added defensively: "And she belongs to me."

"You're a Boer, aren't you?" asked Guntermann.

"Yes."

"I thought Boers hated the blacks."

Van der Kamp shook his head. "We do not hate blacks. We hate only the Zulus, not because they are black but because they are the enemies of our blood."

"And it gets very lonely out here during the long rains, eh?" chuckled Guntermann with a knowing wink.

"Sometimes," said Van der Kamp, still defensive.

"When the British make this land a protectorate," continued Guntermann, "they're going to tell you to get rid of her."

"I've had dealings with the English before," said Van der Kamp grimly. "They do not frighten me."

"May I respectfully suggest that we keep politics out of our discussion, gentlemen?" said Rice. "There's no reason for nationalism out here in the bush."

"Agreed," said Guntermann. He gestured toward Sloane with a smile. "In the interests of international unity, perhaps we should ask our American colleague to remove his military uniform."

"You can ask," said Sloane.

Rice studied the outfit for a moment.

"I see you were a captain, sir," noted the Englishman.

Sloane shook his head. "Nope."

"But your insignia—"

"I bought this outfit after the war."

"Then you didn't see any action?"

Sloane paused before answering. "I saw my share of it."

"Which side were you on?" asked Rice.

"I thought we were supposed to avoid politics," noted Sloane.

Rice loosened a couple of buttons on his shirt and began fanning himself again. "This isn't politics, it's just curiosity," persisted the Englishman. "Why did you choose to buy a Confederate uniform? After all, they lost."

"Reflects the sun more, shows the dust less," answered Sloane.

"And is this hat that which your American cowboys wear?" asked Guntermann, pointing to Sloane's stetson.

"You'd have to ask an American cowboy."

Guntermann threw back his head and laughed. "Well said, sir! By the way, we haven't been introduced. I'm Erhard Guntermann, and this gentleman is Blaney Rice."

"Hannibal Sloane."

"*The* Hannibal Sloane?" asked Rice, raising his voice as the chorus of hippos started up once again.

"Unless there are two of us."

"Your reputation precedes you, sir," said Rice. "You're said to be one of the most successful ivory hunters in East Africa."

"One of 'em," agreed Sloane.

"They mention you in the same breath with Selous and Karamojo Bell," said the Englishman, obviously impressed.

"Never met them," said Sloane.

"How many elephants have you killed?" asked Rice.

Sloane finished rolling his cigarette and lit it up.

"A few," he said at last.

"You're being modest."

"Possibly he's the strong, silent type," said Guntermann with an amused smile.

"Possibly," said Sloane.

"Actually," continued the German, "while I don't doubt your accomplishments, the very best elephant hunter of all is less than 50 feet away from this bar at this very minute."

"The big Lumbwa with the hand-axe?" asked Sloane.

The German smiled. "The very one! Have you ever seen a native hunt elephant with an axe?"

"Once," said Sloane.

"This one—Tumo is his name—is the best," said the German proudly.

"Are you suggesting that he can actually kill an elephant with a hand-axe?" asked Rice skeptically.

"With ease."

"I hate to call you on it," said the Englishman, "but I've hunted a few elephant in my day, and I simply don't believe you."

"I have seen him kill eleven elephants with no weapon but his axe," said Guntermann.

Rice stared thoughtfully at his glass. "Perhaps in the rain forest, where they don't have any maneuvering room," he mused. "Perhaps there—but surely not out here on the savannah!"

"Anywhere," said the German adamantly.

"You're not talking about females or totos?" said Rice, turning to Guntermann. "You're stating that he can bring down a full-grown bull elephant?"

"That is correct."

Rice shook his head. "It can't be done."

"I have seen it done many times," replied Guntermann.

"A six-ton elephant, with nothing but a hand-axe?"

The German nodded emphatically.

"I don't want to call you a liar," said Rice, "but I'm willing to wager that it can't be done."

"Name your price," said the German confidently.

The Englishman pulled a wad of notes out of his wallet, counted them off, and laid them on the bar. "How about fifty pounds?"

"Certainly," agreed Guntermann. He smiled confidently at Rice. "How about one hundred pounds?"

"That's an awful lot of money."

"Either he can kill the elephant or he can't," said the German. "The amount of the bet will not effect the outcome." He paused. "Of course, if you'd rather not..."

Rice counted out another fifty pounds. "Done!"

"I accept!" said the German happily. He rummaged through his pockets and pulled out an equivalent amount in marks and Maria Theresa dollars. He pushed both piles of money toward Van der Kamp. "You can hold the stakes."

The Boer nodded his agreement, picked up the money, and tucked it into a pocket.

"There's one condition," said Rice.

"Oh?"

"He's got to make his kill tomorrow. I'm due in Kampala five days from now, and I'll never make it if I don't start tomorrow afternoon."

"That was never mentioned as part of the wager," said the German. "What if we cannot find a bull elephant tomorrow?"

Rice lowered his head in thought, then turned to Sloane. "Mr. Sloane, would you be willing to be my representative on the hunt, to make sure the conditions are fulfilled?"

"It could take days," said Sloane. "And I don't work for free."

"That was never my intention," said Rice. "I'll pay you half my winnings."

Sloane shook his head. "I'll take the ivory."

"But if he doesn't make a kill, there won't be any ivory," noted Rice.

"He'll make the kill."

"What make you so certain?" demanded Rice.

"I told you: I've seen a Lumbwa work with an axe before," answered Sloane.

"How the devil can a man kill an elephant with nothing but a hand-axe?" persisted Rice.

"He'll hamstring him," said the American.

"What do you mean?" insisted Rice.

Sloane turned to Guntermann. "It's your Lumbwa; *you* tell him."

The German smiled coyly. "If I start telling people how he does it, who would bet with me?"

"Well, since I've already put up my money and I won't be here to see it, I'd like *someone* to tell me," said Rice irritably.

"All right," said Sloane. "The Lumbwa will track down the elephant, and approach to within maybe 40 yards. Then he'll wait until the wind is right, sneak up behind him, and sever the tendons of a back leg about a foot above the ground." He turned to the German. "Right?"

Gunterman merely smiled.

"Some animals—a rhino, for example—can get along just fine on three legs," added Sloane, "but an elephant's got to have all four. Hamstringing him nails him to the spot."

"All right," said Rice grudgingly. "That demobilizes him. How does he kill him?"

"All elephants are right-handed or left-handed," said Sloane. "The Lumbwa won't strike until he figures out which side the elephant favors."

"What has *that* got to do with anything?" demanded Rice.

"Once he's hamstrung, the elephant will spin around to the side he favors with his trunk outstretched, trying to locate his attacker. Then the Lumbwa will either hack off the trunk with a single stroke, or put a deep gash in it."

"And then?"

"If he's in the middle of a herd, he'll run for cover; otherwise, he'll just stand twenty feet away and wait for it to bleed to death."

"It sounds gruesome!" said Rice.

"It's not a pretty sight," agreed Sloane. "Once I determine that the elephant's done for, I'll stick a bullet in his ear and put him out of his misery."

"And you're sure the Lumbwa can do this?" said Rice.

"Unless he's clumsy," said Sloane. "Everyone makes a mistake sooner or later."

"If it's as easy as you make it sound, why are there still any elephants left at all?" said Rice bitterly.

"I didn't say it was easy," replied Sloane. "I said it was possible."

"I suppose I might as well concede the bet right now," said Rice.

"No," said Guntermann. "We go hunting tomorrow morning."

"Why bother?" said the Englishman.

"You are not the first man to bet against Tumo," answered the German. "I always give him a brand-new Maria Theresa dollar when he wins my money for me. Why cheat him out of it?"

"Why not just pay him?" suggested Sloane.

"He does not work, he does not get paid," replied Guntermann firmly.

"Besides," said Sloane, "there's always a chance he'll mess it up. If he does, you can pick up your winnings from Van der Kamp next time you come through."

"Say, that's right!" said Rice suddenly. "How many chances does he get? I mean, if he's such a clumsy tracker that he scares the elephant off, does that count?"

"He will require only one chance," said Guntermann. "Once he begins his final close stalk, that is the elephant that we bet on."

"You're willing to make that part of the wager?" asked Rice.

"I am."

Rice ordered another round of beers as the light began to fail and millions of frogs began croaking in the nearby river.

"For all the ivory and half the winnings, I'll take the Lumbwa out alone," offered Sloane. "We can probably travel much faster that way."

"No," objected Guntermann. "I am going too. I love to watch my Lumbwa in action."

"All right," said Sloane. "But just you and him—no entourage. If we start shooting meat for your boys we may scare all the elephants out of the area—and I don't plan to spend a month of my life waiting for one set of ivory."

"Agreed," said the German. "Will you be taking your Kikuyu?"

"He goes where I go."

Guntermann nodded his approval. "Good! We will need two boys to carry back the ivory."

They set out the next morning, the four of them, walking inland from the river. Tumo, the Lumbwa, and Karenja, Sloane's Kikuyu tracker, studiously ignored each other, and Guntermann was nursing a hangover, so they proceeded in total silence for the first two hours. They saw huge herds of wildebeest and gazelle, but nothing larger except for an occasional giraffe, and after another hour they unloaded their packs and rested in the shade of a ten-foot-tall termite mound.

"How soon before we come to elephant spoor?" asked Guntermann, taking a long swallow from his canteen.

"It'll be a while yet," replied Sloane, removing his left shoe and cutting a jigger out from beneath nail of his big toe. "This area's been pretty well shot out. The elephant have moved east and probably a bit north, and they're getting pretty timid."

"Will it be today, do you think?" persisted Guntermann.

"Probably not for two or three days," replied Sloane. "If we're lucky."

"You're sure?"

Sloane shrugged. "You never know. There are always a few lone bulls around, if you're lucky enough to find them, but the rule of thumb for an ivory hunter is that you walk 25 miles for every shot you take, unless you're the type who blows away cows and calves." He paused and swatted a tsetse fly away. "Why? Thinking of going back to the trading post?"

"Rice virtually conceeded the wager," noted Guntermann.

"Whether he conceeded or not is between you and him," said Sloane. "But if I don't get the ivory, I want the money."

"Then we proceed!" snapped Guntermann, getting to his feet.

"Whatever you say," said Sloane, putting on his shoe.

"What are you doing in this area if there is so little ivory here?" asked Guntermann irritably.

"I came back from Uganda for porters," said Sloane. "I got the chief an Acholi village mad at me and had to leave in a hurry. My men all deserted, except for Karenja here."

"I do not understand," said Guntermann. "A tribe of Acholi wants to kill you, and you say you are going back there? Why?"

"I buried three tons of ivory before I left," said Sloane. "Once I hire myself some porters, and maybe a few *askaris* who know how to use their rifles, I'm going back there to dig it up."

"I see," said Guntermann, wiping his face with his ever-present handkerchief. "But why have you come so far for your porters?"

"They're less likely to desert if they don't speak the local language and don't know how to get home," replied Sloane.

They proceeded in silence across the vast plains, spotting some distant herds of impala, zebra and eland, but approaching within 500 yards of nothing except a lone ostrich, which scurried away when it spotted them. When they stopped to eat beneath an acacia tree, a pair of lionesses suddenly appeared and strode past them, no more than 30 yards away, ignoring them with regal disdain. Shortly thereafter a rhino approached them, snorted ferociously, faked a charge, and then trotted off with its tail held high.

By nightfall they had seen thousands of antelope and tens of thousands of birds, but no sign of elephant, and they camped out in a grove of thorn trees while Tumo and Karenja took turns standing guard, surrounded by the night sounds of the veldt: the high-pitched giggling of hyenas, the coughing of a lion on the prowl, the frightened bark of a zebra.

The next morning began as uneventfully as the previous one, but before the sun had risen very high in the sky they came to a pile of elephant dung. Karenja walked up to it, squatted down, and stuck his hand into it.

"*Baridi*, Bwana," he announced as the Lumbwa walked over to examine it.

"What does he say?" asked Guntermann.

"He says it's cold, by which he means that it's old and dry," replied Sloane. "No sense following this one."

"This is ridiculous!" said Guntermann in exasperation as Tumo confirmed Karenja's finding. "Just last year there were thousands of elephants here!"

"They're not houses, Guntermann," said Sloane.

"What does that mean?" snapped the German.

"It means they don't stay put where you find them."

They covered another seven miles, passing several more herds of wildebeest and a large troop of baboons, then settled down for a meal while Tumo, the Lumbwa, went off by himself. He returned excitedly half an hour later, announcing that he had found fresh elephant spoor.

"How many?" asked Sloane.

"Just one," replied Tumo.

"Full-grown?"

The Lumbwa nodded. "Big bull," he said.

"Okay," said Sloane. "It looks like we're in business. Where did you find it?"

The Lumbwa pointed off to the east, and explained that it was less than a mile away.

"No sense sitting around here," said Sloane, loading his pack and picking up his rifle. "You ready, Guntermann?"

The German got to his feet. "Yes."

"Then let's go."

They walked due east for almost a mile, then turned slightly north. Finally the Lumbwa pointed out a fresh pile of elephant dung.

Karenja walked over, examined at it, then looked at the nearby ground and walked back to Sloane, a frown on his handsome face.

"It is *Malima Temboz*, Bwana—The Mountain That Walks," he announced so softly that only Sloane could hear him.

"You're sure?" asked Sloane.

Karenja led him over to the spoor. "You see?" he said, pointing out the twin furrows where the elephant's tusks had plowed up the dry earth as he walked. "The Makonde call him *Bwana Mutaro* because of the furrows he leaves, and my own people know him as *Mrefu Kulika Twiga*, for he is taller than giraffes, but he is truly *Malima Temboz*."

Sloane called Guntermann over.

"Yes, what is it?" asked the German, still excited over finding the fresh spoor.

"Tell your boy that we don't want any part of this elephant," said Sloane. "We'll find another one, and you'll still win your bet."

"Why?" demanded Guntermann. "What is wrong with this one?"

"I know this elephant," explained Sloane. "He's killed more than a dozen natives, including a Wanderobo who was probably every bit as good with an axe as your Lumbwa is."

"You have actually seen him?"

Sloane shook his head. "No. But I've heard about him."

"How can you possibly know this is the same elephant?" scoffed Guntermann.

Sloane led him over to the spoor. "That's the biggest footprint I've ever seen," he said. "Just on size alone, this has to be the same one. And see the way his tusks plow up the ground whenever he walks? That's why they call him *Bwana Mutaro*—Master Furrow. He must be carrying two hundred pounds a side." He paused. "That's a lot of elephant to kill with a hand-axe.

He's an old boy, and he's been around. Your boy isn't going to sneak up on him or catch him napping."

"If he carries so much ivory, why don't you want him?" asked Guntermann.

"I do," replied Sloane. "And now that I know he's in the area, I'll be back for him when this wager is over. But you didn't bargain on sending your boy against *Malima Temboz*. We'll find another one."

"The Mountain That Walks?" repeated Guntermann excitedly. "I want to see this elephant!"

"Maybe someday you will."

"I mean now!"

"I've already explained to you…"

"But if Tumo *does* kill him, think of the publicity!" said Guntermann.

"What publicity?" snorted Sloane. "You're 500 miles from the coast, and 5,000 miles from anyone who cares."

"I will have him stuffed and mounted, and bring them both back to Europe: the world's greatest elephant and the savage who killed him armed only with a hand-axe."

"You're crazy."

"We are wasting time," said Guntermann, ignoring him. "Tumo!" The Lumbwa looked questioningly at him.

"*Kwenda*—let's go!"

The Lumbwa nodded and began trotting alongside the twin furrows in the earth.

Karenja turned to Sloane.

"It's his show," said the American. "Let *him* do the work." He fell into step behind the Lumbwa, followed by Karenja and Guntermann.

They spent the next nine hours traveling in a relatively straight line, occasionally losing the distinctive spoor but always finding it again, then diverted to the east where the elephant had found a small, muddy water hole. Since the full moon was out, the Lumbwa elected to keep following the furrows rather than let the elephant start distancing them, and at daybreak they came to a pile of dung that was less than 20 minutes old.

"We're getting awfully close," said Sloane after calling Guntermann over. "He's probably only a mile or two ahead of us, and since he's been traveling all night there's every chance that he'll sleep as soon as the sun's a little higher. Are you still sure you want to go through with this?"

"Absolutely!" responded the German.

Sloane paused and stared at Guntermann for a long moment, then nodded. "All right," he said. "From here on, we don't talk, cough, hum or whistle. Watch my hand signals, and when I motion you to stop, you obey me instantly. Understand?"

Guntermann nodded.

"I'm going to send Karenja out ahead of us, just in case there are any other elephants in the vicinity who might cause a problem."

"And if he finds some?"

"If he does, he'll come back and let us know how many and where."

Sloane gave his instructions to the Kikuyu, who set off at right angles to them at a fast trot, then nodded to the Lumbwa, who once again began following the spoor, though much more slowly and silently this time.

And then, as they came to a small glade of flowering trees, the Lumbwa stopped, standing stock-still, and Sloane motioned Guntermann to do the same.

The Lumbwa carefully removed his hand-axe. Then, reaching down to a pile of dung, he smeared it all over his body to mask his own odor. He picked up a handful of grass and tested the wind, then silently entered the glade, crouching low, setting each foot down carefully.

Sloane and Guntermann remained where they had stopped for five minutes, then ten more.

"What's taking him so long?" Guntermann whispered, but Sloane merely gestured him to silence and continued staring at the glade. Then a loud trumpeting came to their ears, following by the shrieking of birds and monkeys breaking cover, and then all was silent again.

"Let's go!" muttered Sloane, approaching the glade. He entered the glade carefully, checking every tree, every movement of grass, every fluttering leaf. Guntermann was about to pass him when he reached out an arm and stopped the German.

Finally, after another five minutes, they came to what was left of the Lumbwa—a blood-stained *kikoi* and a pulpy mass that bore no resemblence to a human being. They found his hand-axe fifty yards away. Though Sloane spent another few minutes checking his surroundings, there was no sign of the elephant.

"He's gone," he announced when he was sure they were alone. "I'm sorry about your boy, but I warned you: this isn't just another elephant."

Guntermann shook his head sadly.

"What a tragedy!" he muttered. "I could have toured Europe!"

"I'm glad to see you're so deeply moved," said Sloane sardonically.

Guntermann glared at him. "I have lost one hundred pounds. Isn't that enough?"

Sloane shrugged noncommittally. "If you say so," he replied. There was a crackling of bushes and Sloane leveled his rifle in the direction of the sound, but it was only Karenja, racing up to see what had happened. The Kikuyu read the scene instantly. "*Malima Temboz* knew he was coming," said Karenja, pointing to the ground. "You see, he led him deeper and deeper into the trees, then turned *here*"—he indicated the place—"and silently came back *here*"—he gestured again—"by his trail to lie in wait. Truly he is the wisest and most terrible of elephants!"

Sloane studied Karenja's reconstruction of the scene, then nodded. "He probably never knew the elephant was behind him until it grabbed him." He sighed. "Well, there's nothing left to bury. We might as well be going."

"Where?" asked Guntermann, as they began walking out of the glade. "Back to the trading post?"

"*You're* going back to the trading post," said Sloane. "I've got an elephant to hunt."

"I'm coming with you," said Guntermann firmly.

Sloane shook his head. "Your bet's over and done with. This is business now; you'd only slow me down."

"But I want to see him!"

"Tumo probably saw him—for a couple of seconds, anyway," said Sloane. "Do you think it was worth it?"

Sloane knelt down and examined the pile of dung.

"Dry," he muttered. "You'd think he'd have slowed down by now."

"He is *Malima Temboz*," said Karenja, as if that explained everything.

Sloane leaned up against a dying baobab tree and set to work rolling a cigarette as he scanned the horizon.

"Where's the nearest water?" he asked.

The Kikuyu pointed to the east.

"How far?"

"Half a day," said Karenja. "Maybe more. Maybe less."

"Well, we might as well get going," said Sloane with a grimace. "No reason why he should be the only one to drink today."

They set off beneath the high tropical sun, the Rift Valley behind them, the coast and Mombasa an unimaginable march to the east through hundreds of miles of thorn trees. The ground became so hard that the elephant's tusks no longer plowed it up as he walked, and their rate of pursuit diminished as they twice lost touch with his spoor and had to backtrack to pick it up again. They came to a Wakamba village three hours later, asked if anyone had seen *Malima Temboz*, and received the kind of looks usually reserved for madmen and fools. Sloane pulled three cartridges out of his belt and offered them to anyone who could tell him how recently the elephant had passed by and what direction it had been headed, but there were no takers.

Finally, as night fell, they came to a narrow, dirty river and slaked their thirst, then made camp beneath an acacia tree.

"Terrible place!" muttered Sloane, alternately shivering and slapping at mosquitos.

"The Maasai call it *Nairobi*," Karenja informed him.

"*Nairobi*? What does it mean?"

"The place of cool water."

"The place of a million mosquitos is more like it," grated Sloane.

"We call it the place of cold swamps," added Karenja.

"Well, that's closer, anyway," said Sloane, pulling his blanket over his head, more for protection from the insects than from the chilling breeze that swept across the plain.

Sloane spent an uncomfortable night, getting up twice to add to the fire and wishing that he could strangle the one particular hyena whose high-pitched giggling seemed to rouse him every time that he was on the brink of sleep. He was actually relieved to see the morning come, and, though sleepy and ill-tempered, lost no time breaking camp and taking up his quest once again.

They had been on the trail for no more than half an hour when they came to a flat, dusty plain where a herd of buffalo had obliterated all sign of the elephant.

"Wonderful," growled Sloane. He stood erect, placed his hands on his hips, and surveyed the area. "Which way, do you suppose? South to Tsavo, north to Kikuyuland, or straight ahead?"

"Not to Tsavo, Bwana," said Karenja. "Too dry."

"Lot of elephants down there, though," noted Sloane.

"*Malima Temboz* does not like his own kind. Always he walks alone."

"All right," said Sloane. "Let's turn north and see if we can pick up his trail."

They began walking to the north, examining the ground every few minutes, but after two hours Sloane concluded that the elephant must have headed east or south.

"I do not think so, Bwana," said Karenja. "He is next to a god, so it is logical that he would go to *Kirinyaga*, the mountain where *Ngai* dwells."

"He's just an elephant, Karenja."

"He is *Malima Temboz*."

"Even *Malima Temboz* leaves a spoor," said Sloane. "You've been following it for three days."

Karenja had no answer to that, so he remained silent.

"Let's go back and see where we lost him," continued Sloane.

"*Ndio*, Bwana," agreed Karenja reluctantly.

They backtracked toward the place where the buffalo herd had obliterated the elephant's tracks. At one point a pride of lions blocked their path, huddled about the carcass of a dead eland, and Sloane made a large semi-circle around them through a heavy stand of thorn bush.

"*Bwana!*" whispered Karenja excitedly as they came opposite the pride.

"What is it?"

The Kikuyu pointed toward the ground, where two furrows, about six feet apart, were plainly visible.

Sloane frowned. "Why the hell would he go through bush when there was a plain track to follow?"

"He is *Malima Temboz*," explained Karenja patiently. "Thorns are no more to him that the petals of a flower."

They began following the trail, and came to a pile of dung half a mile later.

"Warm," announced Karenja, stricking two fingers into it.

"How old?"

"Maybe ten minutes. Maybe fifteen. Maybe twelve."

"I'll be damned!" muttered Sloane. "The son of a bitch is stalking *us*!"

"He knows we are here, Bwana," said Karenja. "We came back with heavy feet."

"I know *he's* here, too," said Sloane, "so we're even."

Karenja picked up a handful of dirt and ground it to powder between his fingertips, watching it drift to the north.

"The wind favors *Malima Temboz*, Bwana."

"Then we'll even the odds," said Sloane. He headed off to his left, followed by the Kikuyu. When he had gone half a mile, he turned right and continued walking through the oppressive heat for an hour, until he felt reasonably secure that he was once again ahead of the elephant. He then turned back into the thorn bush, looking for a likely place of concealment. Once there, he sent Karenja up a nearby tree as a lookout, placed two shells in his rifle, and waited.

An hour passed, then another, then a third.

"Any sign of him yet?" asked Sloane without much hope.

"*Hapana*, Bwana."

"You're sure?"

"He is not here."

"All right," said Sloane with a sigh. "Come on down."

Karenja clambered down the tree while Sloane slung his rifle over his sweat-soaked shoulder.

"Let's get out of this bush and back onto the grass," said Sloane.

They walked half a mile to the east, emerging from the scrub thorn onto the broad plain—and almost immediately came upon the elephant's spoor.

"Christ!" snapped Sloane. "He walked right past us while we were sitting in there being eaten by insects!"

He knelt down and examined the furrows. "This is one goddamned smart elephant."

"He is *Malima Temboz*," said Karenja, nodding sagely as if the Bwana had finally realized what Karenja had been saying all along.

Sloane didn't bother to respond, but simply began following the spoor again.

They soon reached a drier, hotter area, free of trees and scrubland, brimful of gazelles and zebra and impala and wildebeest. Sloane sought out a nearby termite mound, climbed to the top of it, reached into his pack, and pulled out his spyglass.

"I've got him!" he announced a moment later.

"Where?" asked Karenja.

Sloane pointed off to the northeast.

"Are you certain it is *Malima Temboz*?"

"He's too far away to see his ivory," answered Sloane. "But he's a big one, and he's traveling alone."

He jumped down from the mound.

"All right," he said. "We know he likes to play games, so let's see if we can't outsmart him this time. See that grove of trees about six miles ahead?"

"*Ndio*, Bwana," said Karenja, nodding.

"If he thinks we're still after him, he's going to lie up and wait for us there."

"He is not a lion, to lie in wait," said Karenja.

"He's not your run-of-the-mill elephant, either," said Sloane. "He knows he's being followed, and he knows he's more vulnerable out on the grass. He'll head for the trees, believe me." He paused, wiping some dust from his eyes. "You go off to the right and circle around that grove. If he breaks out, I want to know which way he's going."

"And you, Bwana?"

"I'm going straight into the trees. There's a waterhole about four miles ahead and maybe a mile to the left; if he stops to drink and take a mud bath, I think I can beat him to the grove."

"And if he does not stop to drink?"

"Then I'll go in after him. You give a holler if you see him break cover."

Karenja held out his hand. "*Kwaheri*, Bwana."

"What do you mean, Good-bye?" said Sloane. "I'll see you in two hours."

"*Ndio*, Bwana," said the Kikuyu without much conviction. Then he set off at a trot.

Sloane looked across the plain, tried without success to spot the huge bulk of the elephant, took a sip of water from his canteen, and began walking toward the distant grove of trees. Herds of gazelle and impala scattered out of his way and he slowed his pace, not wanting to alert the elephant to his presence. Soon he found the right rate of speed, and was able to walk past the grazing animals without distressing them. He was just congratulating himself on the ease with which he had crossed the plain when he found a lone rhino blocking his path.

It peered at him, snorting, then began trotting in a large semi-circle until it was able to get his wind. Sloane slowly unslung his rifle and laid it across his chest, hoping that he wouldn't have to use it and reveal his presence to the elephant. The rhino came to a stop about sixty yards away, then began pawing the earth and snorting vigorously. A moment later it trotted to within twenty yards of him, then cut away at a right angle.

Sloane remained motionless, and the rhino circled him again, obviously troubled by his scent. Once again the animal lowered its head and charged, and once again it veered off when twenty yards away. Finally, shaking its head furiously, it turned its back on him and galloped away, burping violently from both ends.

Sloane waited another minute to make sure that it wouldn't be returning, then continued his trek toward the glade of trees. As he approached them, the animals became more skittish, possibly because the trees offered cover for carnivores, and began racing off as he approached them. He checked the ground for signs of the elephant's spoor, saw none, and slowly began circling to his left, hoping that he might be able to spot the elephant on the open plain.

He had gone almost a third of the way around the glade when he heard Karenja's voice call out.

"Bwana, he has gone back into the trees!"

"Back *into* them?" muttered Sloane to himself. "How the hell did he get here without my seeing him?"

He checked his cartridges, placed two extras between the fingers of his left hand, and entered the glade, which he estimated to be about two hundred yards in diameter.

Twenty feet into the trees he stopped, and listened for telltale signs: the rumbling of the elephant's stomach, the breaking of a twig, anything to help pinpoint the animal's location. He heard nothing, and after another moment he walked in another twenty feet. Again he stood still, and again he heard nothing but the trilling of birds and the chirping of crickets. He wanted to yell to Karenja, to see if the elephant had emerged again, but he didn't dare give away his own location, and so, foot by foot, he continued walking through the glade. Visibility was rarely more than ten feet, frequently five, and he suddenly became aware of the idiocy of tracking *Malima Temboz* through such dense cover. He quickly retraced his steps, and emerged into the open with an enormous sense of relief.

Now he stood back some fifty yards and called out to Karenja: "Is he still in the glade?"

"Ndio, Bwana!"

"Wait about ten minutes for him to forget I'm here, and then start making noise on your side. Maybe we can frighten him out in this direction."

"He is not afraid of noise, Bwana!" yelled Karenja.

"Do it anyway!"

Karenja made no reply, but about fifteen minutes later he began beating the branches of the trees and screaming at the top of his lungs, while Sloane, kneeling, rifle in hands, scanned the length of the glade, waiting for the elephant to burst out.

Nothing happened.

The noise stopped ten minutes later, and half an hour after that Karenja timidly circled the glade and approached Sloane.

"What are you doing here?" demanded the hunter.

"I thought you must be dead, Bwana, for I heard no shots," explained Karenja, "so I came to take your body to the missionaries."

"Thanks," said Sloane sardonically.

"Shall I go back to beating the branches, Bwana?"

Sloane shook his head. "No, that doesn't seem to do any good."

"Then what shall we do?"

"Wait," said Sloane. He tapped his canteen meaningfully. "We've got more water than he does. That water hole is a mile away; sooner or later he has to come out."

"Sooner or later men must sleep."

"Always the optimist," said Sloane.

"Shall I go back to the other side, Bwana?"

"Yes, I think so. And take this with you"—he handed Karenja the spyglass—"just in case he sneaked out while you were over here talking to me."

Karenja took the glass and headed off at a trot, while Sloane pulled his pack off and took out a piece of biltong and began chewing laboriously on it. Day turned to twilight, and twilight to evening, and still the elephant remained hidden within the glade. Finally Sloane decided that it was too dark to see, so he built a large fire, more to aim by than to keep the carnivores away, and sat down beside it, his back propped up against his pack, his rifle laid gently across his legs.

A lion coughed in the distance and a herd of wildebeest stirred uneasily about half a mile to the west. Somewhere a leopard roared and an antelope screamed, and then all was silent again.

And then, instinctively, Sloane looked up—and there, charging as silently as the night, with no scream, no warning trumpet, was *Malima Temboz*.

The hunter raised his rifle to his shoulder and stared at the great beast. Its huge ears blotted out the moon and stars, its enormous bulk made the earth shake with each step it took, its twin pillars of ivory seemed to extend to Eternity.

"You're everything they said you were!" murmured Sloane, staring awestruck as the elephant bore down upon him.

At the last possible instant he got off a shot. The bullet raised a swirl of dust on the elephant's skull, but didn't stop him, or even slow him down, as Sloane had somehow known it wouldn't.

He continued staring in wonder as the thick trunk and shining ivory reached out for him. It was, he decided, a sight that could last a man a lifetime.

And a lifetime was all he had left.

Karenja found what was left of his Bwana a few minutes later. He waited until morning and buried the tattered gray outfit, and then, because he had seen the way white men treated their dead, he placed a cross upon the grave and carefully hung Sloane's weather-worn stetson atop it.

Then he went back to his village, paid a large reparation to his chief, bought a wife, and spent the rest of his years tending his goats, for once a man has hunted *Malima Temboz* there are no challenges left to him.

WHAT I DID ON MY SUMMER VACATION

Neither George Laskowski nor I could figure out why the readers of Lan's Lantern, *a science fiction publication, were so enthusiastic about my first safari diary...but when George heard that I was going back again, he insisted upon Part 2.*

August 27-30: Conspiracy turned out to be a far more pleasant worldcon than I had anticipated. I spent most of the time letting the people from Arrow, my British publisher, tell me what a fine fellow I am.

August 31: We met my father, who was accompanying us to Kenya, and boarded a British Airways 747 jetliner from London to Nairobi. It was the last plane in which I would feel safe for quite some time.

September 1: Perry Mason, our private guide, was waiting at the airport to pick us up. In the process he had inadvertantly locked his keys inside his safari car, and it took us about half an hour to fish them out. It made for an informal beginning, anyway. After checking in at the Norfolk Hotel, traditional jumping-off point for Roosevelt's, Hemingway's, Ruark's, and Resnick's safaris, we spent the morning visiting some friends at the East African Wildlife Society, where I autographed some British editions of my books and arranged for the purchase of a photograph that will be the frontespiece to *Ivory*, a novel of mine that Tor will be bringing out just before the 1988 worldcon. Then we stopped by the Jamia Mosque, a couple of bookstores, and the MacMillan Library (which has the finest collection of Africana extant.)

After a quick lunch, we drove to the Nairobi National Park, a 44-square-mile game sanctuary within the city limits, and managed to see four of Kenya's handful of remaining rhinos. (Poachers have lowered their Kenyan population from 23,000 in 1973 to about 400 as I write this; they will almost certainly be extinct in the wild by the year 2000.)

We had dinner at the Carnivore, which remains my favorite Kenyan restaurant. It's fashioned after the open-pit restaurants of Brazil, and any given night a dozen game animals are roasting over the huge fire. Waiters come by every two or three minutes, offering the diners a slice of impala, gazelle, eland, kongoni, or whatever. Fascinating place. (I might add that diners are encouraged not to ask how they come by all these game animals in a country where game ranching is virtually nonexistent and hunting has been outlawed since 1977.)

September 2: We had the Norfolk pack us a batch of box lunches, loaded them into the back of the safari car, and headed north toward the Aberdares Mountains. Along the way we stopped at Thika, where we visited the Blue Posts Hotel (made famous in Elspeth Huxley's *The Flame Trees of Thika*) and photographed the Chania Falls, a beautiful waterfall in downtown Thika where a number of sequences for the Tarzan TV show were shot.

Just outside Thika is Ol Donyo Sabuk, a mountain that has become a national park. It was here that Sir Northrup MacMillan (who later donated the MacMillan Library to Nairobi) had his estate. When he died in 1927 he requested that he be buried at the summit of the mountain, which is only some 6,000 feet high. But MacMillan was built like a typical science fiction fan—he went about 400 pounds after a diet—and after three unsuccessful attempts to carry the coffin up the mountain, they decided to bury him at the foot of the mountain instead. Wise decision, especially since legend has it that on one of those attempts the body fell completely out of the casket and rolled down about 800 feet before it came to rest against a tree. I wish I had been there for the funeral procession; the mind boggles.

The Aberdares mountain range is, for my money, the loveliest section of Kenya, except perhaps for the coast. We drove up to 13,000 feet through heavy forests, had our picnic surrounded by the few remaining black-and-white colobus monkeys, saw some buffalo and bushbuck on our descent, and wound up at the Aberdares Country Club. The former manager of the place, a white British colonial, and his chauffer, a black Kikuyu, were opposing officers during the Mau Mau Emergency a third of a century ago; they later became very close friends, bound together by a shared experience which shaped their lives more than any other. (And yes, their thinly-disguised analogs will be featured prominently in a forthcoming novel.)

September 3: We drove north through the frontier town of Isiolo, which used to be the jumping-off point for all serious elephant hunts, and is now the dividing line between the "secure" section of Kenya and that which is at the mercy of gangs of armed Somali bandits—and soon pulled into Buffalo Springs, Carol's favorite spot in the world. It's a harsh, savage, arid semi-desert, and anything you see walking around—lions, elephants, Samburu tribesman—have paid their dues. Darwin would be pleased with this place, because anything that's not fit doesn't make it to noon.

It's north of the Tana River, and for reasons unknown, it seems that all the prettiest varieties of game occur north of the Tana. South of it you get the common zebra; north of it you get the pinstriped Grevy's zebra. South of it you get the Maasai giraffe, its spots all kind of blotchy; north of it you get the Reticulated giraffe, its spots beautifully-outlined. North of the Tana you also get the gerunuk, which hasn't quite made up its mind whether to be a giraffe or a gazelle, and spends most of its life standing on its hind legs, feeding off the tops of bushes.

We stayed in luxury tents, complete with dressing rooms and bathrooms, and while I was sitting just outside the entrance to my tent before dinner, I found myself staring into the bloodshot little eyes of a full-grown 150-pound male baboon, who was squatting no more than 10 feet away from me. Just behind him were perhaps 40 more members of his troop. Others were perched atop my father's tent.

I slowly and carefully pulled my video camera out of its bag and began focusing, trying not to think of all those stories about packs of baboons going suddenly and totally berserk and pulling men and even leopards apart. Then one of the chefs emerged from the mess tent and tossed some garbage into a pit, and suddenly I was watching the start to the Kentucky Derby. I never saw so many animals move so rapidly or so efficiently in my life; Seattle Slew would have been left at the post. Ten minutes later they were back, joining me in the shade of my tent while awaiting their next round of garbage-picking. Interesting animals, albeit lacking a little something in the way of table manners.

September 4: Since it tends to be over 100 degrees in the Northern Frontier District, we decided to begin our morning game run at 6:00 AM and eat breakfast when we returned at 9:30, a practice we were to adopt for the remainder of the safari. We saw herds of elephant and oryx, plus a number of other species, and returned just in time to witness another feeding frenzy by the baboons. They were finally dispersed by the camp's pet ostrich, who chased them all away and then stopped by the bar to cadge drinks from the customers.

After lunch we were entertained by some Samburu dancers. The men were all in their late teens and early twenties, but the girls were no more than eleven or twelve years old. When my father asked about the discrepancy in ages, we explained that most of the twenty-year-old girls had been married for eight or nine years and were busy working on their sixth or seventh baby. It was his introduction to the fact that there is more difference between Africa and America than the animals and the landscape.

Perry found an inordinate number of animals in the afternoon, including a pair of lions that were resting at the roadside, no more than ten feet from where we parked our car to photograph them. Upon returning we found that the staff, aided by the ostrich, had gone to war with the baboons, and had fought them to a draw (which only meant that the garbage stayed in the pit until the hyenas came for it at night. Africa has a marvelous disposal system.)

September 5: Our next stop was the Meru National Park, far and away the least frequented of Kenya's major parks. Perry had been preparing us for it for two days, telling us horror stories about the lodge, but when we arrived we found that they had hired a new manager a couple of months earlier and that it was absolutely beautiful: flowers everywhere, excellent food, and a view of literally hundreds of elephants and thousands of buffalo and plains game from our private balcony.

In the afternoon we took a game run (i.e., a 3-hour ride through the park in the safari car), and came upon the five white rhinos which Kenya imported from South Africa. These are *much* larger than the native black rhinos, and tame as cattle. Originally there were nine of them, but poachers got three the first week, and a fourth a few years later; the remaining five are kept under armed guard 24 hours a day, and are so docile that we were able to walk right up to them and pet them, a stunt you should try with a black rhino only if you are a] suicidal and b] criminally over-insured. (Incidentally, black rhinos aren't black and white rhinos aren't white. They're both gray. The white rhino gets his name from the Afrikanner "vid", for "wide", indicating his square mouth; the black rhino gets his name simply to show that he's different from the "vid" rhino, which everyone pronounces white rhino. Bet you were dying to know that.)

September 6: We took a standard game run in the morning, then decided to drive down to the Tana River (some 25 miles south of us, but a 90-minute drive over the terrain). We saw swarms of hippos in the river, then drove a little way and came to Adamson's Falls (named for former Meru game warden George Adamson, husband of Joy, who wrote all those books about Elsa the lionesss). I'm a waterfall junkie, and I must admit that these were the prettiest of the dozen or so I've seen in Kenya.

September 7: After four days in the semi-desert of the Northern Frontier District, we thankfully pulled up to the Mount Kenya Safari Club, arguably the only 5-star hostelry in all of Africa's game parks, where we were given a 2-bedroom cottage (each with a sunken ceramic tile bath and 2 shower heads). The bedrooms were connected by an enormous living room that contained a pair of sofas, a wet bar, and a fireplace—and given the altitude (7,500 feet) and the fact that this was Kenya's winter, we actually needed the fireplace at night. The toilet wasn't working, but years of running the kennel has made a handyman out of me, and I didn't even charge William Holden's estate for fixing it.

In the afternoon we stopped by the Club's animal orphanage, which along with numerous other species ranging from bushbabies to a 1,200-pound tortoise, now contains 14 bongo, perhaps five percent of the world's population. (Their range was always limited to Mount Kenya and the Aberdares, and most of them were killed for food during the Mau Mau Emergency, when 90% of the war was fought in the mountains.)

September 8: In the morning we decided to drive up to the snowline (about 14,000 feet) of Mount Kenya. At one point Perry stopped the car and explained that he saw his first action right at that spot. (He had originally come to Kenya in 1952 to fight the Mau Mau.) It was densely forested, and as he explained it, he had led a punitive expedition composed of Wanderobo and Samburu warriors up the mountain to pinpoint the location of a particular Mau Mau group. They camped at this spot for the night, and Perry ordered a couple of them to sit up on watch. He awoke in the middle of the night when he heard noises in the bushes. The guards had fallen asleep, and, fearing an attack, he immediately pulled out his gun and opened fire in the direction of the noise. Pandemonium reigned for the next couple of minutes, and when they decided that the invading Mau Mau were either dead or fled, they went gingerly into the bushes—and found a dead hyena with 22 slugs in its body. (In fact, that may have been the genesis of Perry's next career: he was a white hunter from 1958 to 1977.) In the afternoon Carol and I stopped by the stable to rent some horses to ride up the mountain, but they refused to give me one. They had a policy that, because of the altitude and the terrain, no horse was allowed to carry over 190 pounds, and while I'm not in Northrup MacMillan's class, I do top 200. So we spent the rest of the afternoon sitting in our lounge chairs, sipping cold drinks and watching half a hundred varieties of birds, ranging from huge maribous and crested cranes to tiny weavers and plovers, frolicking on the vast lawn.

September 9: We drove from Mount Kenya to Nairobi, then hopped a 5-seater and flew through some disconcertingly choppy wind currents to the far end of the Maasai Mara, where more than a million wildebeest had just migrated from the Serengeti Plains in Tanzania. We stayed at Governor's Camp, a tented camp which possessed electricity but refused to run it into the tents on the assumption that it was more romantic to fumble around in the dim light of a kerosine lamp than to see what you were doing. This made fixing our toilet—right: it didn't work—virtually impossible, and we finally got the manager to send for a plumber from the local Maasai village a few miles away. (He was pretty good, as African plumbers go; it finally worked after only his third visit.)

We only had time for a brief game run before dinner, but managed to see about half a million wildebeest. The wildebeest, it is said, resembles a horse that was put together by committee. I might add that it is somewhat less intelligent than a potted plant. Ugly, stupid, and relatively defenseless—and yet it remains the most successful animal in East Africa, with numbers that must be seen to be fully comprehended. Its survival trick is that every wildebeest cow calves within a couple of weeks of each other in April, and with more than a million babies on the ground, the predators can't quite eat them all, and perhaps 200,000 survive to adulthood, which more than matches the annual adult die-off caused by sickness, old age and predation.

September 10: We took two long, incredibly dusty game runs, during which time I decided that one could easily paraphrase Spiro Agnew when speaking of wildebeest: if you've seen one, you've seen 'em all. I mean, after watching damned near 10,000 wildebeest race off like bats out of hell just because the first one in line got stung by a bee, and watching them all come to a stop as if nothing had happened because the first one happened to run out of breath, you begin to lose any

admiration you may have had for these plug-ugly
luncheons on legs.

We did manage to see a cheetah and her 5
eight-week-old cubs, all of them looking as if Walt
Disney had drawn them, and spent half an hour or so
photographing them as they played like kittens, and we
saw perhaps 10 prides of lions, all grown disgustingly
fat on wildebeest, and we saw some elephants and some
giraffe and some zebra and some Grant's and Thomson's
gazelle, but my overwhelming memory is of the
megaherd of wildebeest stretching as far as the eye
could see.

That night we were entertained by some local
Maasai mucisians. Each night, as we wandered off to
our tents, we were accompanied by an armed (with a
spear) guard who shone a flashlight along the path to
our tent so we wouldn't step where we shouldn't, like on
a hyena. This particular night we heard a rustling in
the bushes about 50 yards from our tent; the guard
turned his flashlight toward the movement, and we saw
a solitary elephant peacefully feeding his face.

A few minutes later there was an enormous
commotion in the camp. It seems that one of the
musicians, instead of accompanying the rest of his group
at the end of the performance, stayed behind for a
couple of beers, lost his flashlight, and, somewhat tipsy,
began walking after them—and bumped into the
elephant, which, startled, ran one tusk through his leg
and the other through his torso, and then threw him up
against a tree. Initially they thought he was dead, but
he was still breathing, and so they loaded him into a
truck and began driving across the Mara to the town of
Narok some three hours away, from which he could be
transported to Nairobi. He was still in intensive care
when we left the Mara, and I don't know to this day
whether or not he survived. (Which simply goes to show
that, even in the game parks and even in the 1980s, the
old African truism still exists: Everything Bites. In fact,
I am reminded that the closest Harry Selby, Robert

Ruark's favorite white hunter, ever came to death was not from a lion or a leopard or an elephant, but from, of all things, a zebra.)

September 11: We spent all day looking for rhinos and hippos. We found the hippos. We also found (i.e., could not get away from) a million wildebeest, all acting like idiots. I found myself really getting sick of the damned things.

September 12: We took off for Nairobi in a 5-seater. As we finished crossing over the Rift Valley, which is perhaps 60 miles wide at that point, Karen Blixen's beloved Ngong Hills came into view.
　"Lovely, aren't they?" I commented.
　"No," muttered Perry, who I suspect does not like flying under even the best of conditions.
　"Why not?" I asked.
　"Because we're looking *up* at them, and we're supposed to be flying *over* them."
　Even the pilot seemed surprised to be looking uphill at them, and finally we skimmed around them...barely.
　We had lunch at the Carnivore, stopped by the Railway Cemetary while Carol and I looked at the headstones—almost everyone there had died from lion, leopard, or cholera—and then drove back into the Rift Valley to Lake Naivasha, where we stayed at the Lake Hotel (which had been the Sparks Hotel, the center of Rift Valley social life, during colonial times.) It was still typically British, which meant that we were shagged out of the restaurant after dessert so that we could have our tea on the beautifully-manicured lawn. The local farmers had been drawing water from Lake Naivasha for irrigation purposes, so not only had much of the bird life left, but we found that we could walk from the hotel to Crescent Island (which may shortly be re-named Crescent Peninsula), where British tradition was being upheld in the form of a polo match.

The Lake Hotel was also the first hotel where our beds were supplied with—and needed—mosquito netting. The game parks have so many lizards crawling around that you never see an insect...but exquisite colonial hotels won't tolerate lizards, and this was the result.

September 13: A day of rest. We drove back to Nairobi, and parted from Perry, who drove on to Mombasa to meet us the next day. Carol decided to spend the afternoon loafing in the Norfolk, but my father and I went to the Nairobi Museum, where among other things we saw the remains of Ahmed of Marsabit, the huge tusker who was protected by Presidential Decree until his death from old age in 1974. After an hour or so we walked across street to the Snake Park, where we saw black and green mambas, rock pythons, Nile crocodiles, and a pair of ancient torsoises engaged in the delicate act of procreation (an act that had commenced before we arrived, and was still going strong when we left an hour later). Since we had no wheels, we decided to eat at the Norfolk's Ibis Grill, and I have now concluded that the food there is even better than at the Carnivore. Not as much fun, but better.

September 14: We showed up at the Nairobi airport to take a jet to Mombasa, found that the line on the left was for the people who had been scheduled to fly to Mombasa the night before except that the plane hadn't been working, finally got our boarding passes, and had a somewhat unsteady flight to Mombasa, Kenya's exotic coastal city. We checked in at the truly luxurious Nyali Beach Hotel (which sprawls over some 48 beautifully-landscaped acres), grabbed some lunch (**warning:** *never* eat African pizza!), and then went into town, where we toured Fort Jesus, the Portugese fort that had been erected in 1590 and was in constant use, as either a fort or a jail, until 1958. We stopped by Ali's Curio Shop, our favorite gift shop on the Kenya coast, which has taken over the old police building and proudly displays the old wooden gallows.   We visited with Big-Hearted Ali and his exceptionally friendly staff for awhile, until it became too hot: Ali will bargain on everything he sells, with one exception—he won't come down a penny on his cold drinks, and he makes a fortune on them because he refuses to ventillate his building, primarily because it would cut into his cold drink business. After driving through the Old City—and one really does expect to come face-to-face with Peter Lorre and Sydney Greenstreet at every corner—we went back to the hotel, ate a candlelight dinner on the beach, watched some local acrobats, and crawled under our mosquito netting.

September 15: We drove off early in the day, cruised by the Aga Khan's and the late Jomo Kenyatta's almost endless seaside estates, took a ferry across Kalifi Creek (one of our most evocative experiences, with smells and sights and drumbeats straight out of a B movie), and after a couple of hours reached the Gedi Ruins, the remains of an Arab city that was built in the 1200s, deserted in 1500, repopulated in 1525, and deserted for good in 1600. There were houses, mosques, shops—some of them standing empty since before Columbus discovered America. Numerous questions remain unanswered: why was the town deserted *twice*, why was it built more than a mile from the ocean when all the other ruins (and there are many of them in Kenya) are on the beach, why are there no signs of warfare? (Yes, these and other questions will be answered—sort of—in an upcoming science fiction novel.)

We left Gedi at about noon and drove north another 15 miles to Malindi, a formerly jumping coastal town which had been very popular with German and Italian tourists until the twin spectres of crime and AIDS turned it into a virtual ghost town. We stayed at the Sindbad Hotel, which would not look out of place as a set piece in *Road To Morocco*. In the afternoon we walked into town, which is not unlike running the gauntlet at a worldcon huckster's room—street vendors were everywhere. Most wanted to sell me their carvings and their trinkets and their postcards, but a few wanted to buy my Banana Republic hat and one of them made me an exceptionally handsome offer for Carol.

Carol did find an Italian dressmaker hidden among the hucksters, and for less than $150 picked up a suit and a dress that would have cost over $1,000 in the States. She spent the rest of the trip trying to think of ways to sneak the dressmaker out of the country in our luggage.

The Sindbad had an open-air bar that was right out of Somerset Maugham's *Rain*. It also had two restaurants. That night we tried to get into the fancier one, only to find that the door, which was composed of 6-inch steel bars, was locked. (The next night we demanded that the manager let us in and asked why the door was locked; he explained that he had locked it to keep out the rain. Think about it.)

We awoke at six in the morning, to find that our toilet, which had worked the previous day, was not functioning. (I realize that by this time I may seem somewhat obsessed by toilets. Sorry about that.) We went down to the desk to complain, and the manager explained that there was nothing wrong with the toilet. To conserve water, he turned the toilets off at midnight and reactivated them at nine in the morning.

"But the shower and the sink worked," I noted. "I tried them, just to see if the water had been shut off."

"Of course they work."

"Then why shut off the toilet?" I demanded.

He smiled. "Who takes a shower at four in the morning?" he responded.

Kenya may belong to the Third World. The Sindbad Hotel belongs to a world all its own.

September 16: After another trip to Carol's dressmaker, we spent most of the morning driving through the back country looking for a natural wonder called Hell's Kitchen. Never did find it, though Perry and I are convinced that at one point we were within three miles of it.

In the afternoon we went to the Marine National Park, a section of the coral reef where Kenya has forbidden fishing and all other forms of what may be termed oceanographic exploitation, rented a glass-bottom boat, and went out looking at fish and coral. Carol had never snorkeled before, but she became a die-hard fan of the sport that afternoon, and I have been informed that we're having an underwater vacation next winter before we return to Africa.

In the evening we were entertained by some local dancers, and the manager broke down and left the toilets on all night.

September 17: This was the day that the God of Transportation frowned upon us—or snickered; I'm still not sure which.

Our next destination was Lamu Island, which has never had a car on it (well, just one car, anyway: the governor's), and Perry therefore had to leave the safari car to the tender mercies of the Sindbad. We were to take a cab to the local airstrip and then hop a five-seater to Lamu, about 80 miles north of Malindi.

It was raining when the cab pulled up. It was a 9-year-old Peugeot with no windshield wipers. It had 4 doors, but only two of them worked. And when we headed off for the airport, it got stuck in second gear; the cabbie couldn't upshift to third or downshift to first.

But we made it, and seven of us (our party of four, the pilot, and two bachelor girls from Nairobi) piled into the five-seater. Since I was the tallest and needed the most leg room, I got to sit up front in the co-pilot's chair. As I looked at the panel, I saw that the clock wasn't working. After we took off, I realized that neither fuel guage was working either. It grew stiflingly hot in the overcrowded little plane, so I asked the pilot how to turn on the ventillation.

"You can't," he said. "It doesn't work."

So, with half the instrument panel out, and the ventillation not working, and the plane carrying more passengers than God and Cesna meant for it to carry, we reached an altitude of 6,500 feet—and then I heard a pop, and suddenly I was feeling very well ventillated indeed, and the plane dropped to 4,500 feet in about 20 seconds.

"What the hell happened?" I asked.

The pilot gave me a great big grin. "The window just blew out," he replied. "Best ventillation in the world."

"You didn't have to do it for me," I said nervously as the plane finally leveled off at about 3,500 feet.

Carol leaned forward and began whispering bailout instructions to me, just in case the window had damaged the tail rudders on its maiden voyage into space.

"You mean the plane might not land?" I asked.

She assured me that the plane would most definitely land, but that it might not do so on a runway, and as we made our approach to the island of Manda (since Lamu has no roads, it would be presumptuous to expect an airstrip), I was prepared to hurl myself away from the plane before it burst into flames—but except for bouncing two or three times as it touched down (which the pilot assured us was par for the course) nothing exceptional happened...unless, like Carol, you persist in believing that walking away from it in one piece was exceptional.

We then were transferred to a dhow—an ancient sailing vessel, except that this one possessed a motor—which took us across the bay to Peponi's Hotel. Peponi means "paradise" in Swahili, and this hotel was aptly named: a dozen cottages nestled in among half a hundred palm trees, flowers everywhere, a superb restaurant, a friendly bar, and eight miles of untouched white sand beaches.

In Casablanca everyone comes to Rick's. Well, in Lamu, everyone comes to Peponi's bar—and within half an hour of our arrival we were visiting with Bunny Allen, one of Kenya's most famous white hunters (and now in his eighties) and a number of other old-timers, most of whom Perry had known and worked with at some point in his past.

After lunch we rented a real (non-motorized) dhow and sailed three miles up the coast to Lamu Town, an Arab city that was built in the 14th Century. The streets are so narrow and winding that none of them will accomodate a car, and most of the buildings were erected prior to 1700. So, alas, were the sewers, and while open gutters carrying raw sewage from the houses to the ocean may have been quite advanced for 1500 A.D., let me tell you that it stunk to high heaven in 1987. Most of the streets boasted little piles of excrement, not all of it from the dogs and cats and donkeys that wandered freely from house to house. Still, it was a fascinating little city, and is where most of the truly beautiful carvings—chess sets, ivory and ebony and brass trunks, etc.—come from.

On the way back the God of Transportation had one last crack at us, and hit us with a nasty little monsoon about a mile from Peponi's. We took on a lot of water, and had to do a lot of quick weight-shifting, but we made it unscathed. Relatively.

September 18: We crawled out of our mosquito netting, had breakfast, and embarked on yet another dhow trip, this one to neighboring Manda Island to see the Takwa Ruins, which were just a bit younger than the Gedi Ruins near Malindi.

These were more difficult to reach, however. We floated deeper and deeper into the mangrove swamps of Manda when finally Omar, our skipper, announced that we had run out of tide and that the dhow could proceed no farther. So he and his brothers (he has six of them, all in the dhow biz) waded inland, and after half an hour returned with what he called a canoe, but was much longer and broader and didn't have any paddles. Then, like Humphrey Bogart pulling the *African Queen*, Omar's youngest brother jumped out of the boat, grabbed hold of a rope, and pulled us the last half mile to the ruins. We took off our shoes and socks and disembarked into the water, which led to the mud, which led to a path covered by thousands of fiddler crabs, which led to the ruins.

When I signed the guest book, I noted that no one else had visited the ruins for the past eleven days.

"No tide," explained the curator. "Only Omar is bold enough to come at this time of month." Then he added, "How do you like our fiddler crabs?"

We were visited by another ten-minute monsoon on the way home (they seemed only to strike when we were in Omar's dhow), and as the dhow began foundering Omar quickly shoved a two-by-six plank over the side of the boat opposite the sail and instructed Carol to climb out to the end and sit there to help balance us. She actually enjoyed the experience; the rest of us spent the remainder of the afternoon recovering.

September 19: Perry left before sunrise to go to Malindi, pick up his car, and drive back to Nairobi, and Omar stopped by shortly thereafter to see where he and his brethren could take us. We explained that we had taken pity on all the people who liked to bask in the sunshine and would therefore not take a dhow ride today. I thought he was going to cry—but we never saw another drop of rain, and spent the day loafing on the beach.

That night it got very hot and close—we were, after all, at sea level very near the equator—and I found that I couldn't feel any draft from the overhead fan beneath the mosquito netting, so at midnight I removed the netting. I woke up the next morning with about 50 mosquito bites on my arms and torso...so now I'm waiting (with some anxiety) to see just how effective my anti-malarial pills really were.

September 20: Talk about travel days. We began by taking the dhow to Manda Island, then grabbed a 5-seater that flew to Malindi, took another five-seater to Mombasa, found that the jet to Nairobi was only two hours late (a good sign, airport personnel assured us), finally flew to Nairobi, and transferred to Perry's safari car to drive to the Norfolk. We then did about 3 hours' worth of gift-shopping for relatives and the kennel staff, packed, drove back to the airport, checked our luggage through, ate dinner, and boarded a British 747 to England just after midnight. It was the first flight that had taken off on schedule since the British 747 that had brought us there.

September 21: Carol has trouble with jet lag, so we decided to spend a day in England at the Gatwick Hilton, catching up on sleep. I also phoned Chris Morgan of Arrow and caught up on the Hugo Awards, since we had left just before they were announced. I also found out that Arrow had made a very handsome 5-digit (in pounds, yet) offer for *Ivory*, and that Chris, who had been raised in Zimbabwe, was anxious to read my next African-based science fiction novel.

So now, if you'll excuse me, I've got to go write it.

KIRINYAGA

*I think it was absolutely fitting, given
my love of East Africa, that when I finally
won a Hugo award, it was for a story
about the Kikuyu people of Kenya, and
their attempts to keep faith with their
vanishing traditions. There will be nine
more Kirinyaga stories before the cycle is
done; at press time, five of them have been
written and sold.*

In the beginning, Ngai lived alone atop the
mountain called Kirinyaga. In the fullness of time He
created three sons, who became the fathers of the
Maasai, the Kamba, and the Kikuyu races, and to each
son He offered a spear, a bow, and a digging-stick. The
Maasai chose the spear, and was told to tend herds on
the vast savannah. The Kamba chose the bow, and was
sent to the dense forests to hunt for game. But Gikuyu,
the first Kikuyu, knew that Ngai loved the earth and
the seasons, and chose the digging-stick. To reward him
for this Ngai not only taught him the secrets of the seed
and the harvest, but gave him Kirinyaga, with its holy
fig tree and rich lands.

The sons and daughters of Gikuyu remained on
Kirinyaga until the white man came and took their
lands away, and even when the white man had been
banished they did not return, but chose to remain in the
cities, wearing Western clothes and using Western

machines and living Western lives. Even I, who am a *mundumugu*—a witch doctor—was born in the city. I have never seen the lion or the elephant or the rhinoceros, for all of them were extinct before my birth; nor have I seen Kirinyaga as Ngai meant it to be seen, for a bustling, overcrowded city of three million inhabitants covers its slopes, every year approaching closer and closer to Ngai's throne at the summit. Even the Kikuyu have forgotten its true name, and now know it only as Mount Kenya.

To be thrown out of Paradise, as were the Christian Adam and Eve, is a terrible fate, but to live beside a debased Paradise is infinitely worse. I think about them frequently, the descendants of Gikuyu who have forgotten their origin and their traditions and are now merely Kenyans, and I wonder why more of them did not join with us when we created the Eutopian world of Kirinyaga.

True, it is a harsh life, for Ngai never meant life to be easy; but it is also a satisfying life. We live in harmony with our environment, we offer sacrifices when Ngai's tears of compassion fall upon our fields and give sustenance to our crops, we slaughter a goat to thank him for the harvest.

Our pleasures are simple: a gourd of *pombe* to drink, the warmth of a *boma* when the sun has gone down, the wail of a newborn son or daughter, the footraces and spear-throwing and other contests, the nightly singing and dancing.

Maintenance watches Kirinyaga discreetly, making minor orbital adjustments when necessary, assuring that our tropical climate remains constant. From time to time they have subtly suggested that we might wish to draw upon their medical expertise, or perhaps allow our children to make use of their educational facilities, but they have taken our refusal with good grace, and have never shown any desire to interfere in our affairs.

Until I strangled the baby.

It was less than an hour later that Koinnage, our paramount chief, sought me out.

"That was an unwise thing to do, Koriba," he said grimly.

"It was not a matter of choice," I replied. "You know that."

"Of course you had a choice," he responded. "You could have let the infant live." He paused, trying to control his anger and his fear. "Maintenance has never set foot on Kirinyaga before, but now they will come."

"Let them," I said with a shrug. "No law has been broken."

"We have killed a baby," he replied. "They will come, and they will revoke our charter!"

I shook my head. "No one will revoke our charter."

"Do not be too certain of that, Koriba," he warned me. "You can bury a goat alive, and they will monitor us and shake their heads and speak contemptuously among themselves about our religion. You can leave the aged and the infirm out for the hyenas to eat, and they will look upon us with disgust and call us godless heathens. But I tell you that killing a newborn infant is another matter. They will not sit idly by; they will come."

"If they do, I shall explain why I killed it," I replied calmly.

"They will not accept your answers," said Koinnage. "They will not understand."

"They will have no choice but to accept my answers," I said. "This is Kirinyaga, and they are not permitted to interfere."

"They will find a way," he said with an air of certainty. "We must apologize and tell them that it will not happen again."

"We will not apologize," I said sternly. "Nor can we promise that it will not happen again."

"Then, as paramount chief, *I* will apologize."

I stared at him for a long moment, then shrugged. "Do what you must do," I said.

Suddenly I could see the terror in his eyes.

"What will you do to me?" he asked fearfully.

"I? Nothing at all," I said. "Are you not my chief?" As he relaxed, I added: "But if I were you, I would beware of insects."

"Insects?" he repeated. "Why?"

"Because the next insect that bites you, be it spider or mosquito or fly, will surely kill you," I said. "Your blood will boil within your body, and your bones will melt. You will want to scream out your agony, yet you will be unable to utter a sound." I paused. "It is not a death I would wish on a friend," I added seriously.

"Are we not friends, Koriba?" he said, his ebon face turning an ash gray.

"I thought we were," I said. "But my friends honor our traditions. They do not apologize for them to the white man."

"I will not apologize!" he promised fervently. He spat on both his hands as a gesture of his sincerity.

I opened one of the pouches I kept around my waist and withdrew a small polished stone from the shore of our nearby river. "Wear this around your neck," I said, handing it to him, "and it shall protect you from the bites of insects."

"Thank you, Koriba!" he said with sincere gratitude, and another crisis had been averted.

We spoke about the affairs of the village for a few more minutes, and finally he left me. I sent for Wambu, the infant's mother, and led her through the ritual of purification, so that she might conceive again. I also gave her an ointment to relieve the pain in her breasts, since they were heavy with milk. Then I sat down by the fire before my *boma* and made myself available to my people, settling disputes over the ownership of chickens and goats, and supplying charms against demons, and instructing my people in the ancient ways.

By the time of the evening meal, no one had a thought for the dead baby. I ate alone in my *boma*, as befitted my status, for the *mundumugu* always lives and eats apart from his people. When I had finished I wrapped a blanket around my body to protect me from the cold and walked down the dirt path to where all the other *bomas* were clustered. The cattle and goats and chickens were penned up for the night, and my people, who had slaughtered and eaten a cow, were now singing and dancing and drinking great quantities of *pombe*. As they made way for me, I walked over to the caldron and took a drink of *pombe*, and then, at Kanjara's request, I slit open a goat and read its entrails and saw that his youngest wife would soon conceive, which was cause for more celebration. Finally the children urged me to tell them a story.

"But not a story of Earth," complained one of the taller boys. "We hear those all the time. This must be a story about Kirinyaga."

"All right," I said. "If you will all gather around, I will tell you a story of Kirinyaga." The youngsters all moved closer. "This," I said, "is the story of the Lion and the Hare." I paused until I was sure that I had everyone's attention, especially that of the adults. "A hare was chosen by his people to be sacrificed to a lion, so that the lion would not bring disaster to their village. The hare might have run away, but he knew that sooner or later the lion would catch him, so instead he sought out the lion and walked right up to him, and as the lion opened his mouth to swallow him, the hare said, 'I apologize, Great Lion.'

"'For what?' asked the lion curiously.

"'Because I am such a small meal,' answered the hare, 'For that reason, I brought honey for you as well.'

"'I see no honey,' said the lion.

"'That is why I apologized,' answered the hare. 'Another lion stole it from me. He is a ferocious creature, and says that he is not afraid of you.'

"The lion rose to his feet. 'Where is this other lion?' he roared.

"The hare pointed to a hole in the earth. 'Down there,' he said, 'but he will not give you back your honey.'

"'We shall see about that!' growled the lion.

"He jumped into the hole, roaring furiously, and was never seen again, for the hare had chosen a very deep hole indeed. Then the hare went home to his people and told them that the lion would never bother them again."

Most of the children laughed and clapped their hands in delight, but the same young boy voiced his objection.

"That is not a story of Kirinyaga," he said scornfully. "We have no lions here."

"It *is* a story of Kirinyaga," I replied. "What is important about the story is not that it concerned a lion and a hare, but that it shows that the weaker can defeat the stronger if he uses his intelligence."

"What has that to do with Kirinyaga?" asked the boy.

"What if we pretend that the men of Maintenance, who have ships and weapons, are the lion, and the Kikuyu are the hares?" I suggested. "What shall the hares do if the lion demands a sacrifice?"

The boy suddenly grinned. "Now I understand! We shall throw the lion down a hole!"

"But we have no holes here," I pointed out.

"Then what shall we do?"

"The hare did not know that he would find the lion near a hole," I replied. "Had he found him by a deep lake, he would have said that a large fish took the honey."

"We have no deep lakes."

"But we do have intelligence," I said. "And if Maintenance ever interferes with us, we will use our intelligence to destroy the lion of Maintenance, just as the hare used his intelligence to destroy the lion of the fable."

"Let us think how to destroy Maintenance right now!" cried the boy. He picked up a stick and brandished it at an imaginary lion as if it were a spear and he a great hunter.

I shook my head. "The hare does not hunt the lion, and the Kikuyu do not make war. The hare merely protects himself, and the Kikuyu do the same."

"Why would Maintenance interfere with us?" asked another boy, pushing his way to the front of the group. "They are our friends."

"Perhaps they will not," I answered reassuringly. "But you must always remember that the Kikuyu have no true friends except themselves."

"Tell us another story, Koriba!" cried a young girl.

"I am an old man," I said. "The night has turned cold, and I must have my sleep."

"Tomorrow?" she asked. "Will you tell us another tomorrow?"

I smiled. "Ask me tomorrow, after all the fields are planted and the cattle and goats are in their enclosures and the food has been made and the fabrics have been woven."

"But girls do not herd the cattle and goats," she protested. "What if my brothers do not bring all their animals to the enclosure?"

"Then I will tell a story just to the girls," I said.

"It must be a long story," she insisted seriously, "for we work much harder than the boys."

"I will watch you in particular, little one," I replied, "and the story will be as long or as short as your work merits."

The adults all laughed and suddenly she looked very uncomfortable, but then I chuckled and hugged her and patted her head, for it was necessary that the children learned to love their *mundumugu* as well as hold him in awe, and finally she ran off to play and dance with the other girls, while I retired to my *boma*.

Once inside, I activated my computer and discovered that a message was waiting for me from

Maintenance, informing me that one of their number would be visiting me the following morning. I made a very brief reply—*"Article II, Paragraph 5"*, which is the ordinance forbidding intervention—and lay down on my sleeping blanket, letting the rhythmic chanting of the singers carry me off to sleep.

I awoke with the sun the next morning and instructed my computer to let me know when the Maintenance ship had landed. Then I inspected my cattle and my goats—I, alone of my people, planted no crops, for the Kikuyu feed their *mundumugu*, just as they tend his herds and weave his blankets and keep his *boma* clean—and stopped by Simani's *boma* to deliver a balm to fight the disease that was afflicting his joints. Then, as the sun began warming the earth, I returned to my own *boma*, skirting the pastures where the young men were tending their animals. When I arrived, I knew the ship had landed, for I found the droppings of a hyena on the ground near my hut, and that is the surest sign of a curse.

I learned what I could from the computer, then walked outside and scanned the horizon while two naked children took turns chasing a small dog and running away from it. When they began frightening my chickens, I gently sent them back to their own *boma*, and then seated myself beside my fire. At last I saw my visitor from Maintenance, coming up the path from Haven. She was obviously uncomfortable in the heat, and she slapped futilely at the flies that circled her head. Her blonde hair was starting to turn grey, and I could tell by the ungainly way she negotiated the steep, rocky path that she was unused to such terrain. She almost lost her balance a number of times, and it was obvious that her proximity to so many animals frightened her, but she never slowed her pace, and within another ten minutes she stood before me.

"Good morning," she said.

"Jambo, Memsaab," I replied.

"You are Koriba, are you not?"

I briefly studied the face of my enemy; middle-aged and weary, it did not appear formidable. "I am Koriba," I replied.

"Good," she said. "My name is—"

"I know who you are," I said, for it is best, if conflict cannot be avoided, to take the offensive.

"You do?"

I pulled the bones out of my pouch and cast them on the dirt.

"You are Barbara Eaton, born of Earth," I intoned, studying her reactions as I picked up the bones and cast them again. "You are married to Robert Eaton, and you have worked for Maintenance for nine years." A final cast of the bones. "You are 41 years old, and you are barren."

"How did you know all that?" she asked with an expression of surprise.

"Am I not the *mundumugu*?"

She stared at me for a long minute. "You read my biography on your computer," she concluded at last.

"As long as the facts are correct, what difference does it make whether I read them from the bones or the computer?" I responded, refusing to confirm her statement. "Please sit down, Memsaab Eaton."

She lowered herself awkwardly to the ground, wrinkling her face as she raised a cloud of dust.

"It's very hot," she noted uncomfortably.

"It is very hot in Kenya," I replied.

"You could have created any climate you desired," she pointed out.

"We *did* create the climate we desired," I answered.

"Are there predators out there?" she asked, looking out over the savannah.

"A few," I replied.

"What kind?"

"Hyenas."

"Nothing larger?" she asked.

"There *is* nothing larger anymore," I said.

"I wonder why they didn't attack me?"

"Perhaps because you are an intruder," I suggested.

"Will they leave me alone on my way back to Haven?" she asked nervously, ignoring my comment.

"I will give you a charm to keep them away."

"I'd prefer an escort."

"Very well," I said.

"They're such ugly animals," she said with a shudder. "I saw them once when we were monitoring your world."

"They are very useful animals," I answered, "for they bring many omens, both good and bad."

"Really?"

I nodded. "A hyena left me an evil omen this morning."

"And?" she asked curiously.

"And here you are," I said.

She laughed. "They told me you were a sharp old man."

"They were mistaken," I replied. "I am a feeble old man who sits in front of his *boma* and watches younger men tend his cattle and goats."

"You are a feeble old man who graduated with honors from Cambridge and then acquired two postgraduate degrees from Yale," she replied.

"Who told you that?"

She smiled. "You're not the only one who reads biographies."

I shrugged. "My degrees did not help me become a better *mundumugu*," I said. "The time was wasted."

"You keep using that word. What, exactly, *is* a *mundumugu*?"

"You would call him a witch doctor," I answered. "But in truth the *mundumugu*, while he occasionally casts spells and interprets omens, is more a repository of the collected wisdom and traditions of his race."

"It sounds like an interesting occupation," she said.

"It is not without its compensations."

"And *such* compensations!" she said with false enthusiasm as a goat bleated in the distance and a young man yelled at it in Swahili. "Imagine having the power of life and death over an entire Eutopian world!"

So now it comes, I thought. Aloud I said: "It is not a matter of exercising power, Memsaab Eaton, but of maintaining traditions."

"I rather doubt that," she said bluntly.

"Why should you doubt what I say?" I asked.

"Because if it were traditional to kill newborn infants, the Kikuyus would have died out after a single generation."

"If the slaying of the infant arouses your disapproval," I said calmly, "I am surprised Maintenance has not previously asked about our custom of leaving the old and the feeble out for the hyenas."

"We know that the elderly and the infirm have consented to your treatment of them, much as we may disapprove of it," she replied. "We also know that a newborn infant could not possibly consent to its own death." She paused, staring at me. "May I ask why this particular baby was killed?"

"That *is* why you have come here, is it not?"

"I have been sent here to evaluate the situation," she replied, brushing an insect from her cheek and shifting her position on the ground. "A newborn child was killed. We would like to know why."

I shrugged. "It was killed because it was born with a terrible *thahu* upon it."

She frowned. "A *thahu*? What is that?"

"A curse."

"Do you mean that it was deformed?" she asked.

"It was not deformed."

"Then what was this curse that you refer to?"

"It was born feet-first," I said.

"That's it?" she asked, surprised. "That's the curse?"

"Yes."

"It was murdered simply because it came out feet-first?"

"It is not murder to put a demon to death," I explained patiently. "Our tradition tells us that a child born in this manner is actually a demon."

"You are an educated man, Koriba," she said. "How can you kill a perfectly healthy infant and blame it on some primitive tradition?"

"You must never underestimate the power of tradition, Memsaab Eaton," I said. "The Kikuyu turned their backs on their traditions once; the result is a mechanized, impoverished, overcrowded country that is no longer populated by Kikuyu, or Maasai, or Luo, or Wakamba, but by a new, artificial tribe known only as Kenyans. We here on Kirinyaga are true Kikuyu, and we will not make that mistake again. If the rains are late, a ram must be sacrificed. If a man's veracity is questioned, he must undergo the ordeal of the *githani* trial. If an infant is born with a *thahu* upon it, it must be put to death."

"Then you intend to continue to kill any children that are born feet-first?" she asked.

"That is correct," I responded.

A drop of sweat rolled down her face as she looked directly at me and said: "I don't know what Maintenance's reaction will be."

"According to our charter, Maintenance is not permitted to interfere with us," I reminded her.

"It's not that simple, Koriba," she said. "According to your charter, any member of your community who wishes to leave your world is allowed free passage to Haven, from which he or she can board a ship to Earth." She paused. "Was the baby you killed given such a choice?"

"I did not kill a baby, but a demon," I replied, turning my head slightly as a hot breeze stirred up the dust around us.

She waited until the breeze died down, then coughed before speaking. "You do understand that not everyone in Maintenance may share that opinion?"

"What Maintenance thinks is of no concern to us," I said.

"When innocent children are murdered, what Maintenance thinks is of supreme importance to you," she responded. "I am sure you do not want to defend your practices before the Eutopian Court."

"Are you here to evaluate the situation, as you said, or to threaten us?" I asked calmly.

"To evaluate the situation," she replied. "But there seems to be only one conclusion that I can draw from the facts that you have presented to me."

"Then you have not been listening to me," I said, briefly closing my eyes as another, stronger breeze swept past us.

"Koriba, I know that Kirinyaga was created so that you could emulate the ways of your forefathers—but surely you must see the difference between the torture of animals as a religious ritual and the murder of a human baby."

I shook my head. "They are one and the same," I replied. "We cannot change our way of life because it makes *you* uncomfortable. We did that once before, and within a mere handful of years your culture had corrupted our society. With every factory we built, with every job we created, with every bit of Western technology we accepted, with every Kikuyu who converted to Christianity, we became something we were not meant to be." I stared directly into her eyes. "I am the *mundumugu*, entrusted with preserving all that makes us Kikuyu, and I will not allow that to happen again."

"There are alternatives," she said.

"Not for the Kikuyu," I replied adamantly.

"There *are*," she insisted, so intent upon what she had to say that she paid no attention to a black-and-gold centipede that crawled over her boot. "For example, years spent in space can cause certain physiological and hormonal changes in humans. You noted when I arrived that I am 41 years old and childless. That is true. In fact, many of the women in Maintenance are childless. If you will turn the babies over to us, I am sure we can find families for them. This would effectively remove them from your society without the necessity of killing them. I could speak to my superiors about it; I think that there is an excellent chance that they would approve."

"That is a thoughtful and innovative suggestion, Memsaab Eaton," I said truthfully. "I am sorry that I must reject it."

"But why?" she demanded.

"Because the first time we betray our traditions this world will cease to be Kirinyaga, and will become merely another Kenya, a nation of men awkwardly pretending to be something they are not."

"I could speak to Koinnage and the other chiefs about it," she suggested meaningfully.

"They will not disobey my instructions," I replied confidently.

"You hold that much power?"

"I hold that much respect," I answered. "A chief may enforce the law, but it is the *mundumugu* who interprets it."

"Then let us consider other alternatives."

"No."

"I am trying to avoid a conflict between Maintenance and your people," she said, her voice heavy with frustration. "It seems to me that you could at least make the effort to meet me halfway."

"I do not question your motives, Memsaab Eaton," I replied, "but you are an intruder representing an organization that has no legal right to interfere with our culture. We do not impose our religion or our morality upon Maintenance, and Maintenance may not impose its religion or morality upon us."

"It's not that simple."

"It is precisely that simple," I said.

"That is your last word on the subject?" she asked.

"Yes."

She stood up. "Then I think it is time for me to leave and make my report."

I stood up as well, and a shift in the wind brought the odors of the village: the scent of bananas, the smell of a fresh caldron of *pombe*, even the pungent odor of a bull that had been slaughtered that morning.

"As you wish, Memsaab Eaton," I said. "I will arrange for your escort." I signalled to a small boy who was tending three goats and instructed him to go to the village and send back two young men.

"Thank you," she said. "I know it's an inconvenience, but I just don't feel safe with hyenas roaming loose out there."

"You are welcome," I said. "Perhaps, while we are waiting for the men who will accompany you, you would like to hear a story about the hyena."

She shuddered involuntarily. "They are such ugly beasts!" she said distastefully. "Their hind legs seem almost deformed." She shook her head. "No, I don't think I'd be interested in hearing a story about a hyena."

"You will be interested in *this* story," I told her.

She stared at me curiously, then shrugged. "All right," she said. "Go ahead."

"It is true that hyenas are deformed, ugly animals," I began, "but once, a long time ago, they were as lovely and graceful as the impala. Then one day a Kikuyu chief gave a hyena a young goat to take as a gift to Ngai, who lived atop the holy mountain Kirinyaga. The hyena took the goat between his powerful jaws and headed toward the distant mountain—but on the way he passed a settlement filled with Europeans and Arabs. It abounded in guns and machines and other wonders he had never seen before, and he stopped to look, fascinated. Finally an Arab noticed him staring intently and asked if he, too, would like to become a civilized man—and as he opened his mouth to say that he would, the goat fell to the ground and ran away. As the goat raced out of sight, the Arab laughed and explained that he was only joking, that of course no hyena could become a man." I paused for a moment, and then continued. "So the hyena proceeded to Kirinyaga, and when he reached the summit, Ngai asked him what had become of the goat. When the hyena told him, Ngai hurled him off the mountaintop for having the audacity to believe he could become a man. He did not die from the fall, but his rear legs were crippled, and Ngai declared that from that day forward, all hyenas would appear thus—and to remind them of the foolishness of trying to become something that they were not, He also gave them a fool's laugh." I paused again, and stared at her. "Memsaab Eaton, you do not hear the Kikuyu laugh like fools, and I will not let them become crippled like the hyena. Do you understand what I am saying?"

She considered my statement for a moment, then looked into my eyes. "I think we understand each other perfectly, Koriba," she said.

The two young men I had sent for arrived just then, and I instructed them to accompany her to Haven. A moment later they set off across the dry savannah, and I returned to my duties.

I began by walking through the fields, blessing the scarecrows. Since a number of the smaller children followed me, I rested beneath the trees more often than was necessary, and always, whenever we paused, they begged me to tell them more stories. I told them the tale of the Elephant and the Buffalo, and how the Maasai *elmoran* cut the rainbow with his spear so that it never again came to rest upon the earth, and why the nine Kikuyu tribes are named after Gikuyu's nine daughters, and when the sun became too hot I led them back to the village.

Then, in the afternoon, I gathered the older boys about me and explained once more how they must paint their faces and bodies for their forthcoming circumcision ceremony. Ndemi, the boy who had insisted upon a story about Kirinyaga the night before, sought me out privately to complain that he had been unable to slay a small gazelle with his spear, and asked for a charm to make its flight more accurate. I explained to him that there would come a day when he faced a buffalo or a hyena with no charm, and that he must practice more before he came to me again. He was one to watch, this little Ndemi, for he was impetuous and totally without fear; in the old days, he would have made a great warrior, but on Kirinyaga we had no warriors. If we remained fruitful and fecund, however, we would someday need more chiefs and even another *mundumugu*, and I made up my mind to observe him closely.

In the evening, after I ate my solitary meal, I returned to the village, for Njogu, one of our young men, was to marry Kamiri, a girl from the next village. The bride-price had been decided upon, and the two families were waiting for me to preside at the ceremony.

Njogu, his faced streaked with paint, wore an ostrich-feather headdress, and looked very uneasy as he and his betrothed stood before me. I slit the throat of a fat ram that Kamiri's father had brought for the occasion, and then I turned to Njogu.

"What have you to say?" I asked.

He took a step forward. "I want Kamiri to come and till the fields of my *shamba*," he said, his voice cracking with nervousness as he spoke the prescribed words, "for I am a man, and I need a woman to tend to my *shamba* and dig deep around the roots of my plantings, that they may grow well and bring prosperity to my house."

He spit on both his hands to show his sincerity, and then, exhaling deeply with relief, he stepped back.

I turned to Kamiri.

"Do you consent to till the *shamba* of Njogu, son of Muchiri?" I asked her.

"Yes," she said softly, bowing her head. "I consent."

I held out my right hand, and the bride's mother placed a gourd of *pombe* in it.

"If this man does not please you," I said to Kamiri, "I will spill the *pombe* upon the ground."

"Do not spill it," she replied.

"Then drink," I said, handing the gourd to her.

She lifted it to her lips and took a swallow, then handed it to Njogu, who did the same.

When the gourd was empty, the parents of Njogu and Kamiri stuffed it with grass, signifying the friendship between the two clans.

Then a cheer rose from the onlookers, the ram was carried off to be roasted, more *pombe* appeared as if by magic, and while the groom took the bride off to his *boma*, the remainder of the people celebrated far into the night. They stopped only when the bleating of the goats told them that some hyenas were nearby, and then the women and children went off to their *bomas* while the men took their spears and went into the fields to frighten the hyenas away.

Koinnage came up to me as I was about to leave.

"Did you speak to the woman from Maintenance?" he asked.

"I did," I replied.

"What did she say?"

"She said that they do not approve of killing babies who are born feet-first."

"And what did *you* say?" he asked nervously.

"I told her that we did not need the approval of Maintenance to practice our religion," I replied.

"Will Maintenance listen?"

"They have no choice," I said. "And *we* have no choice, either," I added. "Let them dictate one thing that we must or must not do, and soon they will dictate all things. Give them their way, and Njogu and Kamiri would have recited wedding vows from the Bible or the Koran. It happened to us in Kenya; we cannot permit it to happen on Kirinyaga."

"But they will not punish us?" he persisted.

"They will not punish us," I replied.

Satisfied, he walked off to his *boma* while I took the narrow, winding path to my own. I stopped by the enclosure where my animals were kept and saw that there were two new goats there, gifts from the bride's and groom's families in gratitude for my services. A few minutes later I was asleep within the walls of my own hut.

The computer woke me a few minutes before sunrise. I stood up, splashed my face with water from the gourd I keep by my sleeping blanket, and walked over to the terminal.

There was a message for me from Barbara Eaton, brief and to the point:

> *It is the preliminary finding of Maintenance that infanticide, for any reason, is a direct violation of Kirinyaga's charter. No action will be taken for past offenses.*
>
> *We are also evaluating your practice of euthanasia, and may require further testimony from you at some point in the future.*
>
> *Barbara Eaton*

A runner from Koinnage arrived a moment later, asking me to attend a meeting of the Council of Elders, and I knew that he had received the same message.

I wrapped my blanket around my shoulders and began walking to Koinnage's *shamba*, which consisted of his *boma*, as well as those of his three sons and their wives. When I arrived I found not only the local elders waiting for me, but also two chiefs from neighboring villages.

"Did you receive the message from Maintenance?" demanded Koinnage, as I seated myself opposite him.

"I did."

"I warned you that this would happen!" he said. "What will we do now?"

"We will do what we have always done," I answered calmly.

"We cannot," said one of the neighboring chiefs. "They have forbidden it."

"They have no right to forbid it," I replied.

"There is a woman in my village whose time is near," continued the chief, "and all of the signs and omens point to the birth of twins. We have been taught that the firstborn must be killed, for one mother cannot produce two souls—but now Maintenance has forbidden it. What are we to do?"

"We must kill the firstborn," I said, "for it will be a demon."

"And then Maintenance will make us leave Kirinyaga!" said Koinnage bitterly.

"Perhaps we could let the child live," said the chief. "That might satisfy them, and then they might leave us alone."

I shook my head. "They will not leave you alone. Already they speak about the way we leave the old and the feeble out for the hyenas, as if this were some enormous sin against their God. If you give in on the one, the day will come when you must give in on the other."

"Would that be so terrible?" persisted the chief. "They have medicines that we do not possess; perhaps they could make the old young again."

"You do not understand," I said, rising to my feet. "Our society is not a collection of separate people and customs and traditions. No, it is a complex system, with all the pieces as dependant upon each other as the animals and vegetation of the savannah. If you burn the grass, you will not only kill the impala who feeds upon it, but the predator who feeds upon the impala, and the ticks and flies who live upon the predator, and the vultures and maribou storks who feed upon his remains when he dies. You cannot destroy the part without destroying the whole."

I paused to let them consider what I had said, and then continued speaking: "Kirinyaga is like the savannah. If we do not leave the old and the feeble out for the hyenas, the hyenas will starve. If the hyenas starve, the grass eaters will become so numerous that there is no land left for our cattle and goats to graze. If the old and the feeble do not die when Ngai decrees it, then soon we will not have enough food to go around."

I picked up a stick and balanced it precariously on my forefinger.

"This stick," I said, "is the Kikuyu people, and my finger is Kirinyaga. They are in perfect balance." I stared at the neighboring chief. "But what will happen if I alter the balance, and put my finger *here*?" I asked, gesturing to the end of the stick.

"The stick will fall to the ground."

"And here?" I asked, pointing to a spot an inch away from the center.

"It will fall."

"Thus is it with us," I explained. "Whether we yield on one point or all points, the result will be the same: the Kikuyu will fall as surely as the stick will fall. Have we learned nothing from our past? We *must* adhere to our traditions; they are all that we have!"

"But Maintenance will not allow us to do so!" protested Koinnage.

"They are not warriors, but civilized men," I said, allowing a touch of contempt to creep into my voice. "Their chiefs and their *mundumugus* will not send them to Kirinyaga with guns and spears. They will issue warnings and findings and declarations, and finally, when that fails, they will go to the Eutopian Court and plead their case, and the trial will be postponed many times and reheard many more times." I could see them finally relaxing, and I smiled confidently at them. "Each of you will have died from the burden of your years before Maintenance does anything other than talk. I am your *mundumugu*; I have lived among civilized men, and I tell you that this is the truth."

The neighboring chief stood up and faced me. "I will send for you when the twins are born," he pledged.

"I will come," I promised him.

We spoke further, and then the meeting ended and the old men began wandering off to their *bomas*, while I looked to the future, which I could see more clearly than Koinnage or the elders.

I walked through the village until I found the bold young Ndemi, brandishing his spear and hurling it at a buffalo he had constructed out of dried grasses.

"*Jambo*, Koriba!" he greeted me.

"*Jambo*, my brave young warrior," I replied.

"I have been practicing, as you ordered."

"I thought you wanted to hunt the gazelle," I noted.

"Gazelles are for children," he answered. "I will slay *mbogo*, the buffalo."

"*Mbogo* may feel differently about it," I said.

"So much the better," he said confidently. "I have no wish to kill an animal as it runs away from me."

"And when will you go out to slay the fierce *mbogo*?"

He shrugged. "When I am more accurate." He smiled up at me. "Perhaps tomorrow."

I stared at him thoughtfully for a moment, and then spoke: "Tomorrow is a long time away. We have business tonight."

"What business?" he asked.

"You must find ten friends, none of them yet of circumcision age, and tell them to come to the pond within the forest to the south. They must come after the sun has set, and you must tell them that Koriba the *mundumugu* commands that they tell no one, not even their parents, that they are coming." I paused. "Do you understand, Ndemi?"

"I understand."

"Then go," I said. "Bring my message to them."

He retrieved his spear from the straw buffalo and set off at a trot, young and tall and strong and fearless.

You are the future, I thought, as I watched him run toward the village. *Not Koinnage, not myself, not even the young bridegroom Njogu, for their time will have come and gone before the battle is joined. It is you, Ndemi, upon whom Kirinyaga must depend if it is to survive.*

Once before the Kikuyu have had to fight for their freedom. Under the leadership of Jomo Kenyatta, whose name has been forgotten by most of your parents, we took the terrible oath of Mau Mau, and we maimed and we killed and we committed such atrocities that finally we achieved Uhuru, for against such butchery civilized men have no defense but to depart.

And tonight, young Ndemi, while your parents are asleep, you and your companions will meet me deep in the woods, and you in your turn and they in theirs will learn one last tradition of the Kikuyu, for I will invoke not only the strength of Ngai but also the indomitable spirit of Jomo Kenyatta. I will administer a hideous oath and force you to do unspeakable things to prove your fealty, and I will teach each of you, in turn, how to administer the oath to those who come after you.

There is a season for all things: for birth, for growth, for death. There is unquestionably a season for Utopia, but it will have to wait.

For the season of Uhuru *is upon us.*

FOR I HAVE TOUCHED THE SKY

I think the Kirinyaga stories constitute my best work to date. The first one has appeared all over, and many of my readers are already familiar with it, so I decided to run the second story in the cycle as well. Besides, it's nominated for the Best Novelette Nebula for 1989, and, it's my favorite.

There was a time when men had wings.

Ngai, who sits alone on His throne atop Kirinyaga, which is now called Mount Kenya, gave men the gift of flight, so that they might reach the succulent fruits on the highest branches of the trees. But one man, a son of Gikuyu, who was himself the first man, saw the eagle and the vulture riding high upon the winds, and spreading his wings, he joined them. He circled higher and higher, and soon he soared far above all other flying things.

Then, suddenly, the hand of Ngai reached out and grabbed the son of Gikuyu.

"What have I done that you should grab me thus?" asked the son of Gikuyu.

"I live atop Kirinyaga because it is the top of the world," answered Ngai, "and no one's head may be higher than my own."

And so saying, Ngai plucked the wings from the son of Gikuyu, and then took the wings away from all men, so that no man could ever again rise higher than His head.

And that is why all of Gikuyu's descendants look at the birds with a sense of loss and envy, and why they no longer eat the succulent fruits from the highest branches of the trees.

We have many birds on the world of Kirinyaga, which was named for the holy mountain where Ngai dwells. We brought them along with our other animals when we received our charter from the Eutopian Council and departed from a Kenya that no longer had any meaning for true members of the Kikuyu tribe. Our new world is home to the maribou and the vulture, the ostrich and the fish eagle, the weaver and the heron, and many other species. Even I, Koriba, who am the *mundumugu*—the witch doctor—delight in their many colors, and find solace in their music. I have spent many afternoons seated in front of my *boma*, my back propped up against an ancient acacia tree, watching the profusion of colors and listening to the melodic songs as the birds come to slake their thirst in the river that winds through our village.

It was on one such afternoon that Kamari, a young girl who was not yet of circumcision age, walked up the long, winding path that separates my *boma* from the village, holding something small and gray in her hands.

"*Jambo*, Koriba," she greeted me.

"*Jambo*, Kamari," I answered her. "What have you brought to me, child?"

"This," she said, holding out a young pygmy falcon that struggled weakly to escape her grasp. "I found him in my family's *shamba*. He cannot fly."

"He looks fully-fledged," I noted, getting to my feet. Then I saw that one of his wings was held at an awkward angle. "Ah!" I said. "He has broken his wing."

"Can you make him well, *mundumugu?*" asked Kamari.

I examined the wing briefly, while she held the young falcon's head away from me. Then I stepped back.

"I can make him well, Kamari," I said. "But I cannot make him fly. The wing will heal, but it will never be strong enough to bear his weight again. I think we will destroy him."

"No!" she exclaimed, pulling the falcon back. "You will make him live, and I will care for him!"

I stared at the bird for a moment, then shook my head. "He will not wish to live," I said at last.

"Why not?"

"Because he has ridden high upon the warm winds." "I do not understand," said Kamari, frowning.

"Once a bird has touched the sky," I explained, "he can never be content to spend his days on the ground."

"I will make him content," she said with determination. "You will heal him and I will care for him, and he will live."

"I will heal him and you will care for him," I said. "But," I added, "he will not live."

"What is your fee, Koriba?" she asked, suddenly businesslike.

"I do not charge children," I answered. "I will visit your father tomorrow, and he will pay me." She shook her head adamantly. "This is *my* bird. *I* will pay the fee."

"Very well," I said, admiring her spirit, for most children—and all adults—are terrified of their *mundumugu*, and would never openly contradict or disagree with him. "For one month you will clean my *boma* every morning and every afternoon. You will lay out my sleeping blankets, and keep my water gourd filled, and you will see that I have kindling for my fire."

"That is fair," she said after a moment's consideration. Then she added: "What if the bird dies before the month is over?"

"Then you will learn that a *mundumugu* knows more than a little Kikuyu girl," I said.

She set her jaw. "He will not die." She paused. "Will you fix his wing now?"

"Yes."

"I will help."

I shook my head. "You will build a cage in which to confine him, for if he tries to move his wing too soon, he will break it again and then I will surely have to destroy him."

She handed the bird to me. "I will be back soon," she promised, racing off toward her *shamba*.

I took the falcon into my hut. He was too weak to struggle very much, and he allowed me to tie his beak shut. Then I began the slow task of splinting his broken wing and binding it against his body to keep it motionless. He shrieked in pain as I manipulated the bones together, but otherwise he simply stared unblinking at me, and within ten minutes the job was finished.

Kamari returned an hour later, holding a small wooden cage in her hands.

"Is this large enough, Koriba?" she asked.

I held it up and examined it.

"It is almost too large," I replied. "He must not be able to move his wing until it has healed."

"He won't," she promised. "I will watch him all day long, every day."

"You will watch him all day long, every day?" I repeated, amused.

"Yes."

"Then who will clean my hut and my *boma*, and who will fill my gourd with water?"

"I will carry his cage with me when I come," she replied.

"The cage will be much heavier when the bird is in it," I pointed out.

"When I am a woman, I will carry far heavier loads on my back, for I shall have to till the fields and gather the firewood for my husband's *boma*," she said. "This will be good practice." She paused. "Why do you smile at me, Koriba?"

"I am not used to being lectured to by uncircumcised children," I replied with a smile.

"I was not lecturing," she answered with dignity. "I was *explaining*."

I held a hand up to shade my eyes from the afternoon sun.

"Are you not afraid of me, little Kamari?" I asked.

"Why should I be?"

"Because I am the *mundumugu*."

"That just means you are smarter than the others," she said with a shrug. She threw a stone at a chicken that was approaching her cage, and it raced away, squawking its annoyance. "Someday I shall be as smart as you are."

"Oh?"

She nodded confidently. "Already I can count higher than my father, and I can remember many things."

"What kind of things?" I asked, turning slightly as a hot breeze blew a swirl of dust about us.

"Do you remember the story of the honey bird that you told to the children of the village before the long rains?"

I nodded.

"I can repeat it," she said.

"You mean you can remember it."

She shook her head vigorously. "I can repeat every word that you said."

I sat down and crossed my legs. "Let me hear," I said, staring off into the distance and idly watching a pair of young men tending their cattle.

She hunched her shoulders, so that she would appear as bent with age as I myself am, and then, in a voice that sounded like a youthful replica of my own, she began to speak, mimicking my gestures.

"There is a little brown honey bird," she began. "He is very much like a sparrow, and as friendly. He will come to your *boma* and call to you, and as you approach him he will fly up and lead you to a hive, and then wait while you gather grass and set fire to it and smoke out the bees. But you must *always*"—she emphasized the word, just as I had done—"leave some honey for him, for if you take it all, the next time he will lead you into the jaws of *fisi*, the hyena, or perhaps into the desert where there is no water and you will die of thirst." Her story finished, she stood upright and smiled at me. "You see?" she said proudly.

"I see," I said, brushing away a large fly that had lit on my cheek.

"Did I do it right?" she asked.

"You did it right."

She stared at me thoughtfully. "Perhaps when you die, I will become the *mundumugu*."

"Do I seem that close to death?" I asked.

"Well," she answered, "you are very old and bent and wrinkled, and you sleep too much. But I will be just as happy if you do not die right away."

"I shall try to make you just as happy," I said ironically. "Now take your falcon home."

I was about to instruct her concerning his needs, but she spoke first.

"He will not want to eat today. But starting tomorrow, I will give him large insects, and at least one lizard every day. And he must always have water."

"You are very observant, Kamari."

She smiled at me again, and then ran off toward her *boma*.

She was back at dawn the next morning, carrying the cage with her. She placed it in the shade, then filled a small container with water from one of my gourds and set it inside the cage.

"How is your bird this morning?" I asked, sitting close to my fire, for even though the planetary engineers of the Eutopian Council had given Kirinyaga a climate identical to Kenya's, the sun had not yet warmed the morning air.

Kamari frowned. "He has not eaten yet."

"He will, when he gets hungry enough," I said, pulling my blanket more tightly around my shoulders. "He is used to swooping down on his prey from the sky."

"He drinks his water, though," she noted.

"That is a good sign."

"Can you not cast a spell that will heal him all at once?"

"The price would be too high," I said, for I had forseen her question. "This way is better."

"How high?"

"Too high," I repeated, closing the subject. "Now, do you not have work to do?"

"Yes, Koriba."

She spent the next few minutes gathering kindling for my fire and filling my gourd from the river. Then she went into my hut to clean it and straighten my sleeping blankets. She emerged a moment later with a book in her hand.

"What is this, Koriba?" she asked.

"Who told you that you could touch your *mundumugu's* possessions?" I asked sternly.

"How can I clean them without touching them?" she replied with no show of fear. "What is it?"

"It is a book."

"What is a book, Koriba?"

"It is not for you to know," I said. "Put it back."

"Shall I tell you what I think it is?" she asked.

"Tell me," I said, curious to hear her answer.

"Do you know how you draw signs on the ground when you cast the bones to bring the rains? I think that a book is a collection of signs."

"You are a very bright little girl, Kamari."

"I told you that I was," she said, annoyed that I had not accepted her statement as a self-evident truth. She looked at the book for a moment, then held it up.

"What do the signs mean?"

"Different things," I said.

"What things?"

"It is not necessary for the Kikuyu to know."

"But *you* know."

"I am the *mundumugu.*"

"Can anyone else on Kirinyaga read the signs?"

"Your own chief, Koinnage, and two other chiefs can read the signs," I answered, sorry now that she had charmed me into this conversation, for I could forsee its direction.

"But you are all old men," she said. "You should teach me, so when you all die someone can read the signs."

"These signs are not important," I said. "They were created by the Europeans. The Kikuyu had no need for books before the Europeans came to Kenya; we have no need for them on Kirinyaga which is our own world. When Koinnage and the other chiefs die, everything will be as it was long ago."

"Are they evil signs, then?" she asked.

"No," I said. "They are not evil. They just have no meaning for the Kikuyu. They are the white man's signs."

She handed the book to me. "Would you read me one of the signs?"

"Why?"

"I am curious to know what kind of signs the white men made."

I stared at her for a long minute, trying to make up my mind. Finally I nodded my assent.

"Just this once," I said. "Never again."

"Just this once," she agreed.

I thumbed through the book, which was a Swahili translation of Victorian poetry, selected one at random, and read it to her:

> *Live with me, and be my love,*
> *And we will all the pleasures prove*
> *That hills and valleys, dales and fields,*
> *And all the craggy mountains yields.*
> *There will we sit upon the rocks,*
> *And see the shepherds feed their flocks,*
> *By shallow rivers, by whose falls*
> *Melodious birds sing madrigals.*
>
> *There will I make thee a bed of roses,*
> *With a thousand fragrant posies,*
> *A cap of flowers, and a kirtle*
> *Embroidered all with leaves of myrtle.*
> *A bed of straw and ivy buds,*
> *With coral clasps and amber studs;*
> *And if these pleasures may thee move,*
> *Then live with me and be my love.*

Kamari frowned. "I do not understand."

"I told you that you would not," I said. "Now put the book away and finish cleaning my hut. You must still work in your father's *shamba*, along with your duties here."

She nodded and disappeared into my hut, only to burst forth excitedly a few minutes later.

"It is a *story!*" she exclaimed.

"What is?"

"The sign you read! I do not understand many of the words, but it is a story about a warrior who asks a maiden to marry him!" She paused. "You would tell it better, Koriba. The sign doesn't even mention *fisi*, the hyena, and *mamba*, the crocodile, who dwell by the river and would eat the warrior and his wife. Still, it is a story! I had thought it would be a spell for *mundumugus.*"

"You are very wise to know that it is a story," I said.

"Read another to me!" she said enthusiastically.

I shook my head. "Do you not remember our agreement? Just that once, and never again."

She lowered her head in thought, then looked up brightly.

"Then teach *me* to read the signs."

"That is against the law of the Kikuyu," I said. "No woman is permitted to read."

"Why?"

"It is a woman's duty to till the fields and pound the grain and make the fires and weave the fabrics and bear her husband's children," I answered.

"But I am not a woman," she pointed out. "I am just a little girl."

"But you will become a woman," I said, "and a woman may not read."

"Teach me now, and I will forget how when I become a woman."

"Does the eagle forget how to fly, or the hyena to kill?"

"It is not fair."

"No," I said. "But it is just."

"I do not understand."

"Then I will explain it to you," I said. "Sit down, Kamari."

She sat down on the dirt opposite me and leaned forward intently.

"Many years ago," I began, "the Kikuyu lived in the shadow of Kirinyaga, the mountain upon which Ngai dwells."

"I know," she said. "Then the Europeans came and built their cities."

"You are interrupting," I said.

"I am sorry, Koriba," she answered. "But I already know this story."

"You do not know all of it," I replied. "Before the Europeans came, we lived in harmony with the land. We tended our cattle and plowed our fields, we produced just enough children to replace those who died of old age and disease, and those who died in our wars against the Maasai and the Wakamba and the Nandi. Our lives were simple but fulfilling."

"And then the Europeans came!" she said.

"Then the Europeans came," I agreed, "and they brought new ways with them."

"Evil ways."

I shook my head. "They were not evil ways for the Europeans," I replied. "I know, for I have studied in European schools. But they were not good ways for the Kikuyu and the Maasai and the Wakamba and the Embu and the Kisi and all the other tribes. We saw the clothes they wore and the buildings they erected and the machines they used, and we tried to become like Europeans. But we are not Europeans, and their ways are not our ways, and they do not work for us. Our cities became overcrowded and polluted, and our land grew barren, and our animals died, and our water became poisoned, and finally, when the Eutopian Council allowed us to move to the world of Kirinyaga, we left Kenya behind and came here to live according to the old ways, the ways that are good for the Kikuyu." I paused. "Long ago the Kikuyu had no written language, and did not know how to read, and since we are trying to create a Kikuyu world here on Kirinyaga, it is only fitting that our people do not learn to read or write."

"But what is good about not knowing how to read?" she asked. "Just because we didn't do it before the Europeans came doesn't make it bad."

"Reading will make you aware of other ways of thinking and living, and then you will be discontented with your life on Kirinyaga."

"But *you* read, and you are not discontented."

"I am the *mundumugu*," I said. "I am wise enough to know that what I read are lies."

"But lies are not always bad," she persisted. "You tell them all the time."

"The *mundumugu* does not lie to his people," I replied sternly.

"You call them stories, like the story of the lion and the hare, or the tale of how the rainbow came to be, but they are lies."

"They are parables," I said.

"What is a parable?"

"A type of story."

"Is it a true story?"

"In a way."

"If it is true in a way, then it is also a lie in a way, is it not?" she replied, and then continued before I could answer her. "And if I can listen to a lie, why can I not read one?"

"I have already explained it to you."

"It is not fair," she repeated.

"No," I agreed. "But it is true, and in the long run it is for the good of the Kikuyu."

"I still don't understand why it is good," she complained.

"Because we are all that remain. Once before the Kikuyu tried to become something that they were not, and we became not city-dwelling Kikuyu, or bad Kikuyu, or unhappy Kikuyu, but an entirely new tribe called Kenyans. Those of us who came to Kirinyaga came here to preserve the old ways—and if women start reading, some of them will become discontented, and they will leave, and then one day there will be no Kikuyu left."

"But I don't want to leave Kirinyaga!" she protested. "I want to become circumcised, and bear many children for my husband, and till the fields of his *shamba,* and someday be cared for by my grandchildren."

"That is the way you are supposed to feel."

"But I also want to read about other worlds and other times."

I shook my head. "No."

"But—"

"I will hear no more of this today," I said. "The sun grows high in the sky, and you have not yet finished your tasks here, and you must still work in your father's *shamba* and come back again this afternoon."

She arose without another word and went about her duties.

When she finished, she picked up the cage and began walking back to her _boma_.

I watched her walk away, then returned to my hut and activated my computer to discuss a minor orbital adjustment with Maintenance, for it had been hot and dry for almost a month. They gave their consent, and a few moments later I walked down the long winding path into the center of the village. Lowering myself gently to the ground, I spread my pouchful of bones and charms out before me and invoked Ngai to cool Kirinyaga with a mild rain, which Maintenance had agreed to supply later in the afternoon.

Then the children gathered about me, as they always did when I came down from my _boma_ on the hill and entered the village.

"_Jambo_, Koriba!" they cried.

"_Jambo_, my brave young warriors," I replied, still seated on the ground.

"Why have you come to the village this morning, Koriba?" asked Ndemi, the boldest of the young boys.

"I have come here to ask Ngai to water our fields with His tears of compassion," I said, "for we have had no rain this month, and the crops are thirsty."

"Now that you have finished speaking to Ngai, will you tell us a story?" asked Ndemi.

I looked up at the sun, estimating the time of day.

"I have time for just one," I replied. "Then I must walk through the fields and place new charms on the scarecrows, that they may continue to protect your crops."

"What story will you tell us, Koriba?" asked another of the boys.

I looked around, and saw that Kamari was standing among the girls.

"I think I shall tell you the story of the Leopard and the Shrike," I said.

"I have not heard that one before," said Ndemi.

"Am I such an old man that I have no new stories to tell?" I demanded, and he dropped his gaze to the ground. I waited until I had everyone's attention, and then I began: "Once there was a very bright young shrike, and because he was very bright, he was always asking questions of his father. 'Why do we eat insects?' he asked one day.

"'Because we are shrikes, and that is what shrikes do,' answered his father.

"'But we are also birds,' said the shrike. 'And do not birds such as the eagle eat fish?'

"'Ngai did not mean for shrikes to eat fish,' said his father, land even if you were strong enough to catch and kill a fish, eating it would make you sick.'

"'Have you ever eaten a fish?' asked the young shrike.

"'No,' said his father.

"'Then how do you know?' said the young shrike, and that afternoon he flew over the river, and found a tiny fish. He caught it and ate it, and he was sick for a whole week.

"'Have you learned your lesson now?' asked the shrike's father, when the young shrike was well again.

"'I have learned not to eat fish,' said the shrike. 'But I have another question.'

"'What is your question?' asked his father.

"'Why are shrikes the most cowardly of birds?' asked the shrike. 'Whenever the lion or the leopard appears, we flee to the highest branches of the trees and wait for them to go away.'

"'Lions and leopards would eat us if they could,' said the shrike's father. 'Therefore, we must flee from them.'

"'But they do not eat the ostrich, and the ostrich is a bird,' said the bright young shrike. 'If they attack the ostrich, he kills them with his kick.'

"'You are not an ostrich,' said his father, tired of listening to him.

"'But I am a bird, and the ostrich is a bird, and I will learn to kick as the ostrich kicks,' said the young shrike, and he spend the next week practicing kicking any insects and twigs that were in his way.

"Then one day he came across chui, the leopard, and as the leopard approached him, the bright young shrike did not fly to the highest branches of the tree, but bravely stood his ground.

"'You have great courage to face me thus,' said the leopard.

"'I am a very bright bird, and I not afraid of you,' said the shrike. 'I have practiced kicking as the ostrich does, and if you come any closer, I will kick you and you will die.'

"'I am an old leopard, and cannot hunt any longer,' said the leopard. 'I am ready to die. Come kick me, and put me out of my misery.'

"The young shrike walked up to the leopard and kicked him full in the face. The leopard simply laughed, opened his mouth, and swallowed the bright young shrike.

"'What a silly bird,' laughed the leopard, 'to pretend to be something that he was not! If he had flown away like a shrike, I would have gone hungry today—but by trying to be what he was never meant to be, all he did was fill my stomach. I guess he was not a very bright bird after all.'"

I stopped and stared straight at Kamari.

"Is that the end?" asked one of the other girls.

"That is the end," I said.

"Why did the shrike think he could be an ostrich?" asked one of the smaller boys.

"Perhaps Kamari can tell you," I said.

All the children turned to Kamari, who paused for a moment and then answered.

"There is a difference between wanting to be an ostrich, and wanting to know what an ostrich knows," she said, looking directly into my eyes. "It was not wrong for the shrike to want to know things. It was wrong for him to think he could become an ostrich."

There was a momentary silence while the children considered her answer.

"Is that true, Koriba?" asked Ndemi at last.

"No," I said, "for once the shrike knew what the ostrich knew, it forgot that it was a shrike. You must always remember who you are, and knowing too many things can make you forget."

"Will you tell us another story?" asked a young girl.

"Not this morning," I said, getting to my feet. "But when I come to the village tonight to drink *pombe* and watch the dancing, perhaps I will tell you the story about the bull elephant and the wise little Kikuyu boy. Now," I added, "do none of you have chores to do?"

The children dispersed, returning to their *shambas* and their cattle pastures, and I stopped by Jumal's hut to give him an ointment for his joints, which always bothered him just before it rained. I visited Koinnage and drank *pombe* with him, and then discussed the affairs of the village with the Council of Elders. Finally I returned to my own *boma*, for I always take a nap during the heat of the day, and the rain was not due for another few hours.

Kamari was there when I arrived. She had gathered more wood and water, and was filling the grain buckets for my goats as I entered my *boma*.

"How is your bird this afternoon?" I asked, looking at the pygmy falcon, whose cage had been carefully placed in the shade of my hut.

"He drinks, but he will not eat," she said in worried tones. "He spends all his time looking at the sky."

"There are things that are more important to him than eating," I said.

"I am finished now," she said. "May I go home, Koriba?"

I nodded, and she left as I was arranging my sleeping blanket inside my but.

She came every morning and every afternoon for the next week. Then, on the eighth day, she announced with tears in her eyes that the pygmy falcon had died.

"I told you that this would happen," I said gently. "Once a bird has ridden upon the winds, he cannot live on the ground."

"Do all birds die when they can no longer fly?" she asked.

"Most do," I said. "A few like the security of the cage, but most die of broken hearts, for having touched the sky they cannot bear to lose the gift of flight."

"Why do we make cages, then, if they do not make the birds feel better?"

"Because they make *us* feel better," I answered.

She paused, and then said: "I will keep my word and clean your hut and your *boma*, and fetch your water and kindling, even though the bird is dead."

I nodded. "That was our agreement," I said.

True to her word, she came back twice a day for the next three weeks. Then, at noon on the twenty-ninth day, after she had completed her morning chores and returned to her family's shamba, her father, Njoro, walked up the path to my *boma*.

"*Jambo*, Koriba," be greeted me, a worried expression on his face.

"*Jambo*, Njoro," I said without getting to my feet. "Why have you come to my *boma*?"

"I am a poor man, Koriba," he said, squatting down next to me. "I have only one wife, and she has produced no sons and only two daughters. I do not own as large a shamba as most men in the village, and the hyenas killed three of my cows this past year."

I could not understand his point, so I merely stared at him, waiting for him to continue.

"As poor as I am," he went on, "I took comfort in the thought that at least I would have the bride prices from my two daughters in my old age." He paused. "I have been a good man, Koriba. Surely I deserve that much."

"I have not said otherwise," I replied.

"Then why are you training Kamari to be a *mundumugu?*" he demanded. "It is well known that the *mundumugu* never marries."

"Has Kamari told you that she is to become a *mundumugu?*" I asked.

He shook his head. "No. She does not speak to her mother or myself at all since she has been coming here to clean your *boma*."

"Then you are mistaken," I said. "No woman may be a *mundumugu*. What made you think that I am training her?"

He dug into the folds of his *kikoi* and withdrew a piece of cured wildebeest hide. Scrawled on it in charcoal was the following inscription:

I AM KAMARI

I AM TWELVE YEARS OLD

I AM A GIRL

"This is writing," he said accusingly. "Women cannot write. Only the *mundumugu* and great chiefs like Koinnage can write."

"Leave this with me, Njoro," I said, taking the hide, "and send Kamari to my *boma*."

"I need her to work on my *shamba* until this afternoon."

"Now," I said.

He sighed and nodded. "I will send her, Koriba." He paused. "You are certain that she is not to be a *mundumugu?*"

"You have my word," I said, spitting on my hands to show my sincerity.

He seemed relieved, and went off to his *boma*. Kamari came up the path a few minutes later.

"*Jambo*, Koriba," she said.

"*Jambo*, Kamari," I replied. "I am very displeased with you."

"Did I not gather enough kindling this morning?" she asked.

"You gathered enough kindling."

"Were the gourds not filled with water?"

"The gourds were filled."

"Then what did I do wrong?" she asked, absently pushing one of my goats aside as it approached her.

"You broke your promise to me."

"That is not true," she said. "I have come every morning and every afternoon, even though the bird is dead."

"You promised not to look at another book," I said.

"I have not looked at another book since the day you told me that I was forbidden to."

"Then explain this," I said, holding up the hide with her writing on it.

"There is nothing to explain," she said with a shrug. "I wrote it."

"And if you have not looked at books, how did you learn to write?" I demanded.

"From your magic box," she said. "You never told me not to look at *it.*"

"My magic box?" I said, frowning.

"The box that hums with life and has many colors."

"You mean my computer?" I said, surprised.

"Your magic box," she repeated.

"And it taught you how to read and write?"

"*I* taught me—but only a little," she said unhappily. "I am like the shrike in your story—I am not as bright as I thought. Reading and writing is very difficult."

"I told you that you must not learn to read," I said, resisting the urge to comment on her remarkable accomplishment, for she had clearly broken the law.

Kamari shook her head.

"You told me I must not look at your books," she replied stubbornly.

"I told you that women must not read," I said. "You have disobeyed me. For this you must be punished." I paused. "You will continue your chores here for three more months, and you must bring me two hares and two rodents, which you must catch yourself. Do you understand?"

"I understand."

"Now come into my hut with me, that you may understand one thing more."

She followed me into the hut.

"Computer," I said. "Activate...."

"Activated," said the computer's mechanical voice.

"Computer, scan the hut and tell me who is here with me."

The lens of the computer's sensor glowed briefly.

"The girl, Kamari wa Njoro, is here with you," replied the computer.

"Will you recognize her if you see her again?"

"Yes."

"This is a Priority Order," I said. "Never again may you converse with Kamari wa Njoro verbally or in any known language."

"Understood and logged," said the computer.

"Deactivate." I turned to Kamari. "Do you understand what I have done, Kamari?"

"Yes," she said, "and it is not fair. I did not disobey you."

"It is the law that women may not read," I said, "and you have broken it. You will not break it again. Now go back to your *shamba.*"

She left, head held high, youthful back stiff with defiance, and I went about my duties, instructing the young boys on the decoration of their bodies for their forthcoming circumcision ceremony, casting a counterspell for old Siboki (for he had found hyena dung within his *boma,* which is one of the surest signs of a *thahu,* or curse), instructing Maintenance to make another minor orbital adjustment that would bring cooler weather to the western plains.

By the time I returned to my hut for my afternoon nap, Kamari had come and gone again, and everything was in order.

For the next two months, life in the village went its placid way. The crops were harvested, old Koinnage took another wife and we had a two-day festival with much dancing and *pombe*-drinking to celebrate the event, the short rains arrived on schedule, and three children were born to the village. Even the Eutopian Council, which had complained about our custom of leaving the old and the infirm out for the hyenas, left us completely alone. We found the lair of a family of hyenas and killed three whelps, then slew the mother when she returned. At each full moon I slaughtered a cow—not merely a goat, but a large, fat cow—to thank Ngai for His generosity, for truly He had graced Kirinyaga with abundance.

During this period I rarely saw Kamari. She came in the mornings when I was in the village, casting the bones to bring forth the weather, and she came in the afternoons when I was giving charms to the sick and conversing with the Elders—but I always knew she had been there, for my hut and my *boma* were immaculate, and I never lacked for water or kindling.

Then, on the afternoon after the second full moon, I returned to my *boma* after advising Koinnage about how he might best settle an argument over a disputed plot of land, and as I entered my hut I noticed that the computer screen was alive and glowing, covered with strange symbols. When I had taken my degrees in England and America I had learned English and French and Spanish, and of course I knew Kikuyu and Swahili, but these symbols represented no known language, nor, although they used numerals as well as letters and punctuation marks, were they mathematical formulas.

"Computer, I distinctly remember deactivating you this morning," I said, frowning. "Why does your screen glow with life?"

"Kamari activated me."

"And she forgot to deactivate you when she left?"

"That is correct."

"I thought as much," I said grimly. "Does she activate you every day?"

"Yes."

"Did I not give you a Priority Order never to communicate with her in any known language?" I said, puzzled.

"You did, Koriba."

"Can you then explain why you have disobeyed my directive?"

"I have not disobeyed your directive, Koriba," said the computer. "My programming makes me incapable of disobeying a Priority Order."

"Then what is this that I see upon your screen?"

"This is the Language of Kamari," replied the computer. "It is not among the 1,732 languages and dialects in my memory banks, and hence does not fall under the aegis of your directive."

"Did you create this language?"

"No, Koriba. Kamari created it."

"Did you assist her in any way?"

"No, Koriba, I did not."

"Is it a true language?" I asked. "Can you understand it?"

"It is a true language. I can understand it."

"If she were to ask you a question in the Language of Kamari, could you reply to it?"

"Yes, if the question were simple enough. It is a very limited language."

"And if that reply required you to translate the answer from a known language to the Language of Kamari, would doing so be contrary to my directive?"

"No, Koriba, it would not."

"Have you in fact answered questions put to you by Kamari?"

"Yes, Koriba, I have," replied the computer.

"I see," I said. "Stand by for a new directive."

"Waiting..."

I lowered my head in thought, contemplating the problem. That Kamari was brilliant and gifted was obvious: she had not only taught herself to read and write, but had actually created a coherent and logical language that the computer could understand and in which it could respond. I had given orders, and without directly disobeying them she had managed to circumvent them. She had no malice within her, and wanted only to learn, which in itself was an admirable goal. All that was on the one hand.

On the other hand was the threat to the social order we had labored so diligently to establish on Kirinyaga. Men and women knew their responsibilities and accepted them happily. Ngai had given the Maasai the spear, and He had given the Wakamba the arrow, and He had given the Europeans the machine and the printing press, but to the Kikuyu He had given the digging-stick and the fertile land surrounding the sacred fig tree on the slopes of Kirinyaga.

Once before we had lived in harmony with the land, many long years ago. Then had come the printed word. It turned us first into slaves, and then into Christians, and then into soldiers and factory workers and mechanics and politicians, into everything that the Kikuyu were never meant to be. It had happened before; it could happen again.

We had come to the world of Kirinyaga to create a perfect Kikuyu society, a Kikuyu Utopia: could one gifted little girl carry within her the seeds of our destruction? I could not be sure, but it was a fact that gifted children grew up. They became Jesus, and Mohammed, and Jomo Kenyata—but they also became Tippoo Tib, the greatest slaver of all, and Idi Amin, butcher of his own people. Or, more often, they became Frederich Neitzsche and Karl Marx, brilliant men in their own right, but who influenced less brilliant, less capable men. Did I have the right to stand aside and hope that her influence upon our society would be benign when all history suggested that the opposite was more likely to be true?

My decision was painful, but it was not a difficult one.

"Computer," I said at last, "I have a new Priority Order that supercedes my previous directive. You are no longer allowed to communicate with Kamari under any circumstances whatsoever. Should she activate you, you are to tell her that Koriba has forbidden you to have any contact with her, and you are then to deactivate immediately. Do you understand?"

"Understood and logged."

"Good," I said. "Now deactivate."

When I returned from the village the next morning, I found my water gourds empty, my blanket unfolded, my *boma* filled with the dung of my goats.

The *mundumugu* is all-powerful among the Kikuyu, but he is not without compassion. I decided to forgive this childish display of temper, and so I did not visit Kamari's father, nor did I tell the other children to avoid her.

She did not come again in the afternoon. I know, because I waited beside my hut to explain my decision to her. Finally, when twilight came, I sent for the boy, Ndemi, to fill my gourds and clean my *boma,* and although such chores are woman's work, he did not dare disobey his *mundumugu,* although his every gesture displayed contempt for the tasks I had set for him.

When two more days had passed with no sign of Kamari, I summoned Njoro, her father.

"Kamari has broken her word to me," I said when he arrived. "If she does not come to clean my *boma* this afternoon, I will be forced to place a *thahu* upon her."

He looked puzzled. "She says that you have already placed a curse on her, Koriba. I was going to ask you if we should turn her out of our *boma.*"

I shook my head. "No," I said. "Do not turn her out of your *boma.* I have placed no *thahu* on her yet—but she must come to work this afternoon."

"I do not know if she is strong enough," said Njoro. "She has had neither food nor water for three days, and she sits motionless in my wife's hut." He paused. "Someone has placed a *thahu* on her. If it was not you, perhaps you can cast a spell to remove it."

"She has gone three days without eating or drinking?" I repeated.

He nodded.

"I will see her," I said, getting to my feet and following him down the winding path to the village. When we reached Njoro's *boma* he led me to his wife's hut, then called Kamari's worried mother out and stood aside as I entered. Kamari sat at the farthest point from the door, her back propped against a wall, her knees drawn up to her chin, her arms encircling her thin legs.

"*Jambo*, Kamari," I said.

She stared at me but said nothing.

"Your mother worries for you, and your father tells me that you no longer eat or drink."

She made no answer.

"You also have not kept your promise to tend my *boma*."

Silence.

"Have you forgotten how to speak?" I said.

"Kikuyu women do not speak," she said bitterly. "They do not think. All they do is bear babies and cook food and gather firewood and till the fields. They do not have to speak or think to do that."

"Are you that unhappy?"

She did not answer.

"Listen to my words, Kamari," I said slowly. "I made my decision for the good of Kirinyaga, and I will not recant it. As a Kikuyu woman, you must live the life that has been ordained for you." I paused. "However, neither the Kikuyu nor the Eutopian Council are without compassion for the individual. Any member of our society may leave if he wishes. According to the charter we signed when we claimed this world, you need only walk to that area known as Haven, and a maintenance ship will pick you up and transport you to the location of your choice."

"All I know is Kirinyaga," she said. "How am I to chose a new home if I am forbidden to learn about other places?"

"I do not know," I admitted.

"I don't want to leave Kirinyaga!" she continued. "This is my home. These are my people. I am a Kikuyu girl, not a Maasai girl or a European girl. I will bear my husband's children and till his *shamba,* I will gather his wood and cook his meals and weave his garments, I will leave my parents' shamba and live with my husband's family. I will do all this without complaint, Koriba, if you will just let me learn to read and write!"

"I cannot," I said sadly.

"But *why?*"

"Who is the wisest man you know, Kamari?" I asked.

"The *mundumugu* is always the wisest man in the village."

"Then you must trust to my wisdom."

"But I feel like the pygmy falcon," she said, her misery reflected in her voice. "He spent his life dreaming of soaring high upon the winds. I dream of seeing words upon the computer screen."

"You are not like the falcon at all," I said. "He was prevented from being what he was meant to be. You are prevented from being what you are not meant to be."

"You are not an evil man, Koriba," she said solemnly. "But you are wrong."

"If that is so, then I shall have to live with it," I said.

"But you are asking *me* to live with it," she said, "and that is your crime."

"If you call me a criminal again," I said sternly, for no one may speak thus to the *mundumugu*, "I shall surely place a *thahu* on you."

"What more can you do?" she said bitterly.

"I can turn you into a hyena, an unclean eater of human flesh who prowls only in the darkness. I can fill your belly with thorns, so that your every movement will be agony. I can—"

"You are just a man," she said wearily, "and you have already done your worst."

"I will hear no more of this," I said. "I order you to eat and drink what your mother brings to you, and I expect to see you at my *boma* this afternoon."

I walked out of the hut and told Kamari's mother to bring her banana mash and water, then stopped by old Benimals *shamba*.

Buffalo had stampeded through his fields, destroying his crops, and I sacrificed a goat to remove the *thahu* that had fallen upon his land.

When I was finished I stopped at Koinnage's *boma*, where he offered me some freshly-brewed *pombe* and began complaining about Kibo, his newest wife, who kept taking sides with Shumi, his second wife, against Wambu, his senior wife.

"You can always divorce her and return her to her family's *shamba*," I suggested.

"She cost twenty cows and five goats!" he complained. "Will her family return them?"

"No, they will not."

"Then I will not send her back."

"As you wish," I said with a shrug.

"Besides, she is very strong and very lovely," he continued. "I just wish she would stop fighting with Wambu."

"What do they fight about?" I asked.

"They fight about who will fetch the water, and who will mend my garments, and who will repair the thatch on my hut." He paused. "They even argue about whose hut I should visit at night, as if I had no choice in the matter."

"Do they ever fight about ideas?" I asked.

"Ideas?" he repeated blankly.

"Such as you might find in books."

He laughed. "They are women, Koriba. What need have they for ideas?" He paused. "In fact, what need have any of us for them?"

"I do not know," I said. "I was merely curious."

"You look disturbed," he noted.

"It must be the *pombe*," I said. "I am an old man, and perhaps it is too strong."

"That is because Kibo will not listen when Wambu tells her how to brew it. I really should send her away"—he looked at Kibo as she carried a load of wood on her strong, young back—"but she is so young and so lovely." Suddenly his gaze went beyond his newest wife to the village. "Ah!" he said. "I see that old Siboki has finally died."

"How do you know?" I asked.

He pointed to a thin column of smoke. "They are burning his hut."

I stared off in the direction he indicated. "That is not Siboki's hut," I said. "His *boma* is more to the west."

"Who else is old and infirm and due to die?" asked Koinnage. And suddenly I knew, as surely as I knew that Ngai sits on His throne atop the holy mountain, that Kamari was dead.

I walked to Njoro's *shamba* as quickly as I could. When I arrived, Kamari's mother and sister and grandmother were already wailing the death chant, tears streaming down their faces.

"What happened?" I demanded, walking up to Njoro.

"Why do you ask, when it is you who destroyed her?" he replied bitterly.

"I did not destroy her," I said.

"Did you not threaten to place a *thahu* on her just this morning?" he persisted. "You did so, and now she is dead, and I have but one daughter to bring the bride price, and I have had to burn Kamari's hut."

"Stop worrying about bride prices and huts and tell me what happened, or you shall learn what it means to be cursed by a *mundumugu*!" I snapped.

"She hung herself in her hut with a length of buffalo hide."

Five women from the neighboring *shamba* arrived and took up the death chant.

"She hung herself in her hut?" I repeated.

He nodded. "She could at least have hung herself from a tree, so that her hut would not be unclean and I would not have to burn it."

"Be quiet!" I said, trying to collect my thoughts.

"She was not a bad daughter," he continued. "Why did you curse her, Koriba?"

"I did not place a *thahu* upon her," I said, wondering if I spoke the truth. "I wished only to save her."

"Who has stronger medicine than you?" he asked fearfully.

"She broke the law of Ngai," I answered.

"And now Ngai has taken His vengeance!" moaned Njoro fearfully. "Which member of my family will He strike down next?"

"None of you," I said. "Only Kamari broke the law."

"I am a poor man," said Nioro cautiously, "even poorer now than before. How much must I pay you to ask Ngai to receive Kamari's spirit with compassion and forgiveness?"

"I will do that whether you pay me or not," I answered.

"You will not charge me?" he asked.

"I will not charge you."

"Thank you, Koriba!" he said fervently.

I stood and stared at the blazing hut, trying not to to think of the smoldering body of the little girl inside it.

"Koriba?" said Nioro after a lengthy silence.

"What now?" I asked irritably.

"We did not know what to do with the buffalo hide, for it bore the mark of your *thahu*, and we were afraid to burn it. Now I know that the marks were made by Ngai and not you, and I am afraid even to touch it. Will you take it away?"

"What marks?" I said. "What are you talking about?"

He took me by the arm and led me around to the front of the burning hut. There, on the ground, some ten paces from the entrance, lay the strip of tanned hide with which Kamari had hanged herself, and scrawled upon it were more of the strange symbols I had seen on my computer screen three days earlier.

I reached down and picked up the hide, then turned to Njoro. "If indeed there is a curse on your *shamba*," I said, "I will remove it and take it upon myself, by taking Ngai's marks with me."

"Thank you, Koriba!" he said, obviously much relieved.

"I must leave to prepare my magic," I said abruptly, and began the long walk back to my *boma*. When I arrived I took the strip of buffalo hide into my hut.

"Computer," I said. "Activate."

"Activated."

I held the strip up to its scanning lens.

"Do you recognize this language?" I asked.

The lens glowed briefly.

"Yes, Koriba. It is the Language of Kamari."

"What does it say?"

"It is a couplet:

> *I know why the caged birds die—*
> *For, like them, I have touched the sky.*"

The entire village came to Njoro's *shamba* in the afternoon, and the women wailed the death chant all night and all of the next day, but before long Kamari was forgotten, for life goes on and she was just a little Kikuyu girl.

Since that day, whenever I have.found a bird with a broken wing, I have attempted to nurse it back to health. It always dies, and I always bury it next to the mound of earth that marks where Kamari's hut had been.

It is on those days, when I place the birds in the ground, that I find myself thinking of her again, and wishing that I was just a simple man, tending my cattle and worrying about my crops and thinking the thoughts of simple men, rather than a *mundumugu* who must live with the consequences of his wisdom.

ON ICE CUBES AND LADIES' UNDERWEAR

A lot of self-appointed experts have been giving out advice about how to travel to Africa. Tony Ubelhor's excellent Pulsar *decided to seek out a real expert—me—to set the record straight.*

It doesn't seem to be any secret that Carol and I keep taking trips to Africa. Of late, however, a number of people have come up and asked us what they should know before taking such a trip themselves.

My first inclination is to recommend a good guide book—and then I remember all the things that none of my 43 African guide books mention, and all the things we had to learn for ourselves, and I usually sit down and spend a little time explaining what the modern African tourist *really* has to know.

None of that crap about shots. You want shots? Go to your doctor and tell him you're going to Kenya or Zimbabwe or even Cairo, and he'll be happy to turn you into a human pincushion. Not passports or visas. Just try to get into an African country without them.

Certainly not cameras. A top camera can cost you as much as a two-week safari; I wouldn't begin to know what to tell you. Besides, you can get that out of your Sunday newspaper's travel pages.

But for some strange reason, nobody is willing to talk about ladies' underwear. Except me.

Now, ladies' underwear has always been one of my favorite subjects, ranking right up there next to ladies who don't wear any underwear at all. But, aesthetics aside, it becomes a very practical matter for the African tourist, especially female tourists (or males with *very* peculiar dressing habits).

Why?

Because when you are on the safari trail, you are at the mercy of the camp staff, not only for food and lodging but for laundry. The standard procedure is for the intrepid traveler to leave his dirty laundry at the foot of his bed when he goes out to watch animals in the morning, and for the camp staff to wash it and return it at night.

But most members of any given camp staff are Islamic, and Moslems refuse to touch women's under-garments—which means that ladies who don't bring a little spare Woolite with them are doomed to be *very* uncomfortable after a couple of weeks in the bush. And Fodor's and Fielding's and the rest of the guide books never mention a word about it.

They *do* mention how important it is to make sure that your water has been boiled, since every body of water on the African continent except for Lake Malawi (where almost nobody ever goes anyway) is rife with *bilharzia* and other noxious diseases, each guaranteed to kill you in an exceptionally nasty way.

So okay, you know that you need boiled water, so you mention it to your guide, and he tells you that every safari camp provides you with a carafe of "safe" water by your bedside, and of course the restaurant serves "safe" water too.

So you come in off the safari trail, having spent the past four hours fighting hundred-degree heat and militarily-organized insects just in order to observe a few animals who were peacefully going about their own business, and you ask for a tall glass of cold water, or maybe a Coke. And out it comes, wet and cool, topped with a couple of ice cubes, just for you.

Don't touch it.

You see, the staffs of every safari camp and lodge understand that Europeans (to most Africans, *all* whites are Europeans) have this weird thing about boiled water—but they don't know *why*. So they'll give you a tall glass of boiled water, and since they're only too happy to please their hot and thirsty clients, they'll toss in a couple of ice cubes that they made from the local *bilharzia*-infested stream that morning.

If you're anywhere in Africa, except for a luxury hotel in Nairobi, don't *ever* drink from a glass containing ice cubes without questioning how the ice was made. (Yeah, the guide books overlook *that* little ditty, too.)

The guide books also haven't gotten around to warning you about the Ugandan Student Scam, though the *Wall Street Journal* gave it a front-page story a couple of years ago.

It works like this. You hit a new headquarters city—Nairobi, Harare, Lusaka, Dar Es Salaam, whichever—and as you leave your hotel and go out to do a little shopping or sightseeing, you are immediately approached by an articulate young man. He'll usually ask where you're from, then exclaim about the coincidence that he is going to be attending *your* state's university next fall. He'll also try to put you on the defensive by asking if there is any prejudice against blacks at the school. (After hearing the scam a couple of times, I usually cut it off right here by explaining that if he can't play point guard and hit 85% of his free throws, he might as well forget the whole thing.) Anyway, as the conversation proceeds, he'll get around to telling you his sad story, which is that he is from Uganda, and because of all the killing that is going on there, he can't return home for fear of life and limb, and that he's been accepted by your state university, but is still $200 short of planefare, and could you help him out—and if you've listened to this point, it's damned hard to look the poor kid in the eye and say No. (Unless you're three blocks from your hotel, in which case you've already been approached by four other Ugandan students, and saying No becomes just a tad easier.)

For a while it looked like the poor Ugandan students were going to be out of work, since Uganda's been at peace for a couple of years now, but last time I was in Nairobi they had been replaced by a legion of South African students who looked and sounded exactly like Ugandan students, so I think you can probably be assured of running into *some* student scam. Just walk around them.

Now, in theory, your guide should protect you from these and other pitfalls, but in point of fact if you haven't got a private guide, you're probably on a package tour and are at the mercy of a social director whose entire knowledge of Africa comes out of the same books you didn't bother to read when you signed up for the tour.

Carol and I always try to get our own private guide, but I do understand that this costs somewhat more, and while we believe that it's more than worth the extra money, I also understand that not everyone is in a financial position to make that choice. Which doesn't mean that there aren't important choices to be made when arranging for a package tour.

There happen to be more than 100 companies currently offering package tours to Africa (and that's just in the United States; go to England and West Germany and you can find 200 more.)

So how do you tell which one to choose?

Well, there are a couple of things you should know.

The first is that every company—with the sole exception of Abercrombie and Kent (which is owned by an entrepreneur named Geoffrey Kent, who invented his mythical partner Abercrombie so that the company's name would remind people of Abercrombie and Fitch)—farms out every facet of your tour to local agencies. What this means is that when you buy a tour

from TWA or Lufthansa or Gametrackers or Travcoa or
whoever, you're not buying *their* services; you're paying
them a fee to send you to a tourist company that
operates on the spot. For example, there are only a
dozen reputable photographic safari companies in all of
Tanzania; every one of the hundred-plus companies in
America uses one of the twelve, and the twelve are all
ranked in order of excellence by the Tanzanian
government. But if you don't know that, you don't know
what questions to ask your American packager.

Most tours offer essentially the same package. If
you're going on a typical Kenya safari, you're going to
see Nairobi, the Maasai Mara, Amboseli, a
game-viewing lodge in the mountains, and probably
Samburu or one of the other northern game parks. If
you're going to Egypt, you're going to spend three or
four days in Cairo, and four or five days on a cruise ship
on the Nile. And so on.

But if you'll do a little homework, you'll discover
that there *are* differences. The Kenya government ranks
all the accomodations in the cities and the game parks,
so you should be able to find a tour that will place you in
the most luxurious surroundings (usually for little or no
extra money). Ditto with Egypt: there are 89 boats
crusing the Nile, but only 6 of them get a 5-star rating
from the Egyptian government; the person who doesn't
read the right guide book and insist on one of those six
boats will get pretty much what he deserves. Ditto with
hotels: the Ramses Hilton is the *only* hotel in Cairo
never to have a reported case of dysentary or botulism,
so the tourist who is willing to stay at a different hotel
has placed himself at risk for no reason other than lack
of homework.

Most governments even rate the local tour
companies. My suggestion is that you ask the American
tour companies who they are farming you out to in
which African countries, while simultaneously reading
the various guide books and writing to the countries
themselves to find out who you *want* to be farmed out to.

(And don't bother asking your local travel agency; they
don't know anything except what they read in the
packagers' brochures.) No one would buy a car or a
computer without researching it thoroughly. I am
constantly amazed by the number of unhappy tourists I
run into who simply didn't spend that extra day doing
their homework before spending a few years' savings on
a vacation that they hate.

So where do you really get the low-down info you
need?

Well, there are a number of good guide books (and
no, Fodor's and Fielding's, the two biggest, are not
among them.) Richard Cox's *Kenya & Northern
Tanzania: A Traveler's Guide* is much the best of the
guide books for East Africa; Melissa Shales' *Guide To
Zimbabwe* is the best Zimbabwe guide; Alec Cambbell's
Guide To Botswana is the ultimate Botswana authority;
and so on. Most of them, except for the Cox, are difficult
to obtain, as they are published in England or
Africa—but since the typical safari for two people can
cost between $6,000 and $20,000, it's certainly worth
the effort to hunt them up before finalizing your choices.

Also, some governments—such as Kenya, the
Seychelles and Malawi—will bend over backward to
help you; others, alas, will not respond at all. However,
almost every country has a wildlife society; simply write
off for one of their publications, and you'll find more
material on tours, guides, and guide books than you'll
know what to do with. There is also an association of
about 50 select U.S. travel agents who specialize in
African tours; try to find one in or near your city and go
through him or her. Your typical local travel agency may
be great at booking you into the Hyatt at Maui, or
getting you from Los Angeles to New York on half an
hour's notice, or making your worldcon travel arrange-
ments, but it has no more knowledge of Africa than you
yourself do. The agent will be happy to take your
money, of course, and then farm you out to a company
like Travcoa or Gametrackers, who will take more of

your money and farm you out to their African affiliates, who will take what's left.

So much for generalizations. What more specifics can I give you?

First, don't take a tape recorder, even if you have it just to listen to music. Only take Walkmans.

Why? Because a tape recorder has a microphone and recording capabilities, and that means you're CIA, since no one else has any reason to record anything any resident of the country has to say, and you can count on being hassled for half a day before they finally let you pass through Customs.

(Yes, I know they let video recorders with built-in microphones in without a second glance, but the Third World doesn't always—or even frequently—operate on the same principles of logic that govern the first two.)

Second, only convert *small* amounts of American money or traveler's checks into African currency, especially toward the end of your trip.

Why? Because you are only allowed to take the equivalent of five or ten dollars of African currency out of a country—which means that if you walk up to Customs at the end of a safari with a couple of hundred dollars in Kenya shillings or Zimbabwe dollars or Botswana pulas in your wallet, the Customs officers will confiscate everything above and beyond what you are allowed to take with you.

(Each country also has an exit fee, payable in American money. In Kenya it's twenty dollars, in Tanzania fifty, and so on. *Never* try to pay it with, say, a one-hundred-dollar traveler's check. They'll take it, give you your change in shillings, then explain that you can only take $5.00 worth of shillings with you, and instantly confiscate the rest. Nice work if you can get it.)

Other tips?

Never buy native art in the cities. You can get the same stuff in the bush for a quarter of the price.

Never buy "authentic" Makonde wood carvings unless you've got an expert along to authenticate them.

The Makonde of Tanzania are known far and wide as the greatest wood carvers in East Africa—but if every Makonde who ever lived worked 25 hours a day doing nothing but carving wood, they couldn't produce as many "authentic" Makonde wood carvings as are currently on display in Nairobi alone.

(In fact, if I can put in a plug here, buy most of your Kenyan, Tanzanian and Ugandan trinkets at the East African Wildlife Society's gift shop. It's on the mezzanine level of the Nairobi Hilton, and at least you know that every shilling you spend will go to protect the wildlife you have come to see. You can also join the society and receive *Swara*, their bi-monthly publication, by sending $35.00 to the East African Wildlife Society, P.O. Box 20110, Nairobi, Kenya. They are wonderful, dedicated people, and they'll put the money to good use.)

Haggle. Every listed price is approximately 200% to 300% higher than the seller will settle for. And nothing is so unique that you can't find ten duplicates in the next three shops.

Never talk politics in public. Every sub-Saharan nation claims to be a true democracy, but only Botswana actually is one. You can get in *serious* trouble discussing flaws in the system, even in safari camps out in the bush—and, more important, if you're speaking to a guide or a local, you can get *him* in trouble. After all, he's got to live in this non-democracy after you're safely home wondering why their government doesn't function more like ours.

Don't take flashy jewelry. The average sub-Saharan African makes less than $300 a year, and that Rollex watch or diamond bracelet you're wearing constitutes ten years' worth of income, and one hell of a temptation, to him.

Almost every sub-Saharan country except Kenya has a thriving black market in foreign currency. Don't mess with it. They jail people for that and throw away the keys. Even if you're an American. (And in some places, *especially* if you're an American.)

Remember that you can bring ten tons of stuff *into* an African country without any penalty, but you can only take 44 pounds *out* of it before they start charging you $2.00 a pound for excess weight. So, if you're bringing books to read, bring paperbacks that you can throw away, and if you're buying things, remember that you're going to have to pay extra for them if they're heavy.

(Hint: no one weighs your carry-on bag. We put extra-heavy straps on ours, and usually manage to cram about 60 pounds into each of them. The only hard part is not shuffling like Igor when carrying them through Customs.)

Remember to reconfirm your plane reservations at least three days before you leave. Don't trust your travel agent, your guide, or your hotel's concierge to do it for you. Getting home is more important to you than it is to them, and most African flights oversell by about 20%. (British Airways is the one exception.)

If you are a woman and you're going to an Islamic country (or even an Islamic city such as Mombasa or Lamu), you must cover everything between your neck and your knees, and this includes your back and shoulders. Unless you like riots, that is. (In fact, in Malawi you will actually be arrested if your skirt doesn't cover your knees. Instead of arguing the Right or Wrong of it, you'd be much better to accept the True or False of it and obey the law.)

I suppose what this is all about, in the long run, is not so much Unwritten Rules as Common Sense. Fail to use it and you'll hate your one and only African vacation; apply it and you might find youself going back as often as Carol and I do.

THE END OF THE GAME

My novel, Paradise, *is an allegory of Kenya's history, from about 1880 to about 2010. The last great elephant hunt in East Africa took place in the Lado Enclave in 1910; close to a quarter of a million elephants were butchered in less than six months, and nothing was ever quite the same again. This excerpt, narrated by an old hunter, attempts to show both sides of the incident: the romanticism of the last hunt, and the bloodbath that it truly was. For "Landship" read elephant; for "eyestone" read ivory; and so on.*

What you have to understand about the Bukwa Enclave (said Hardwycke) is that everything came together at once. To begin with, the planetary Governor decided that Peponi was too big for one man to keep tabs on everything, so he divided it up into twelve districts, each with its own District Commissioner. Eleven Commissioners were in place within a month, but the twelfth, the one whose territory included the Bukwa Enclave, was in a hospital halfway across the galaxy and wasn't expected to arrive for almost six months.

Also, a little war had erupted on Columbus II, which was less than two light years away, and about

three-quarters of Peponi's military personal were transferred there for the duration.

Then came the news that the Republic's jewelers
were so desperate for eyestones that they would now
accepts blues and clears.

So what you had was a situation in which the
military was no longer out there enforcing the law, the
Bukwa district had no Commissioner, and you could sell
any eyestone you could take, no matter what color. This
led to virtually an open season on Landships, and the
highest concentration of Landships on the planet was
the Bukwa Enclave, a huge savannah between the
Jupiter Mountains and the Dust Bowl.

Once the word went out that the jewelers were
buying, everyone—and I mean *everyone*—headed up to
the Enclave. It wasn't just the hunters; I mean, hell,
there were never that many of us to begin with. But
hundreds of farmers like Gabe Pickett took off for
Bukwa, and they were joined by miners and traders. I
never saw them, but I heard stories that there were
even some Bluegills up there, operating entirely on their
own.

Catamount Greene was one of the first to arrive.
He'd been living in Berengi, scrounging for credits here
and there, ever since the government made him give up
being the Human King of the Bogoda, and he didn't
know the first thing about tracking, but old Catamount
never let minor details like that stop him. On the way to
the Enclave he stopped by his old stamping grounds and
picked up a bunch of trinkets and jewelry from the
Bogoda, then found one of the few military outposts left
in the Bukwa area and explained that he was trading
Bogoda artifacts to the wags who lived in the Enclave.
He gave a few of the better ones to the soldiers, bought
them a couple of drinks, and went on to say that he was
terrified of Landships and that he had heard that the
Enclave was filled with them—and within ten minutes
he had talked them into marking where the herds were
on a map so that he could avoid them while he hawked

his wares from village to village. He walked into the Enclave with one weapon, three bearers, and his map, and walked out a month later with more than 3,000 eyestones.

Bocci, who had made up his mind to leave Peponi, stuck around just long enough to clean up in the Enclave. He found a water hole way out at the western end, staked it out, poisoned it, and picked up 700 eyestones without ever firing a shot.

Jumping Jimmy Westerly went in with a stepladder, took it out in the shoulder-high grass where none of the other hunters would go, climbed atop it, and potted twenty Landships the first day he was there. Once they cleared out of the area, he followed them, always keeping to high grass. He'd set up his ladder again whenever they stopped, and he kept right on doing it until he had his thousand eyestones.

Other hunters used other methods. Hellfire Bailey brought in a whole tribe of Dorado, who used poisoned spears and arrows and brought down almost three thousand Landships before the new Commissioner finally showed up and the soldiers returned from Columbus II.

After a couple of months, the Enclave began to resemble a war zone, and I don't just mean the piles of Landship carcasses. First of all, a lot of the farmers really didn't know much about hunting, and more than half a hundred of them were killed by Landships. Then, as the Landships themselves started getting harder to find—the ones who survived didn't want to go anywhere near anything that smelled like a Man or a Bluegill—some of the hunters started marking off territories.

Kalahari Jenkins found a dry area, about forty miles square, at the northwestern tip of the Enclave, announced that it was his personal hunting ground, and swore he'd kill anyone who wandered into it. A miner named Kennedy wandered in one day, chasing a couple of Landships, and Jenkins blew him away. What he didn't know was that Kennedy had six sons, and this started a blood feud. Lasted a couple of weeks before they killed him—I seem to remember that he got four of them first—and then the two remaining sons declared that it was now *their* territory. That lasted about five days, until Hakira came up from the south with that damned Demoncat of his. The Demoncat killed the last two Kennedy boys, and Hakira never fired a shot; he just gathered up all of Jenkins' and the Kennedys' eyestones and lit out for Berengi.

Nobody ever found out what happened to the Maracci Sisters. They were damned good hunters, those girls—but one day they just disappeared, both of 'em, and no one ever found the 800 eyestones they were supposed to have taken.

After about five months, word began coming back from Berengi that the price on eyestones had dropped because so many were coming in, so those of us up in the Enclave started going after other stuff as well, Bush Devil skins and anything else that might have a market value. I never did see a Sabrehorn, but they say that Bocci killed the very last one on the planet up in the Enclave.

After a while, even the scavengers couldn't keep up with the abundance of carcasses, and the place became a charnel house, with Landship carcasses everywhere. Some of the Nightkillers got overly bold and started attacking humans, and we damned near had a war on our hands for a while there...but after a while the few remaining packs of Nightkillers went back to eating Landships.

Then the District Commissioner finally arrived. He started making all kinds of pronouncements, but he was powerless to do anything until he got his soldiers back from Columbus, and by then there weren't enough Landships left to make hunting them worthwhile.

When the dust had cleared, the best estimates were that less than five hundred men had gone into the Bukwa Enclave, and that in less than six months three million eyestones had come out. It was the last great hunt, on Peponi or anywhere else, and an awful lot of fortunes were made there. Only about half the men who went in came out, but most of them never had to worry about money again. They took Catamount Greene to court and charged him with poaching. That was nothing new—they were *always* taking him to court over something or other, and he always beat the charges, just like he beat this one. But they took about twelve other hunters to court, including Bocci and Hellfire Bailey, and some of them *didn't* beat the charge. Their money was confiscated, and they were given a choice: five years in jail or take the next ship off Peponi and never come back.

I went to the trials, and as I sat in the back of the courtroom, I realized that we weren't being judged by any jury of our peers. Hell, all of our peers were dead or on trial. I looked around the room, and all I saw were settlers and farmers and merchants, and you could tell just by studying their faces that they found men like Fuentes and Hakira and even Johnny Ramsey an embarrassment. You know how you feel ashamed of the way you used to act when you were a kid? Well, they were ashamed of the men who opened up Peponi. Oh, they knew that what we did was necessary, but you could tell that they had decided times were changing and we had outlived our usefulness.

They even asked the planetary Governor to testify, and he promised in no uncertain terms that he would bring the full power of the government to put an end to poaching. He didn't stop there, either. He announced that he was going to regulate hunting much more carefully, and that Peponi was creating fifteen game parks to go with the one they'd gazetted on the Siboni Plains. He started rattling off the locations, and I realized that I had just been put out of business: every area I had ever hunted was going to become an animal preserve.

It didn't matter much by then, because I already knew it was time to leave. You looked at all those faces and listened to the official pronouncements, and you knew that Peponi was changing too fast. Oh, there'd be hunting for another twenty or thirty years, but it was on the way out. Navy teams were coming in to map out unexplored territories, even the Impenetrable Forest. The hotels didn't want us coming into town and blowing off steam after a safari, and suddenly Main Street was lined with a batch of safari companies that no one had ever heard of, each of them offering their clients seven exotic worlds in less than a Galactic Standard month. They promised to pick a client up at his hotel, fly him right to the edge of a herd of Landships, give him an hour of thrills while he shot his trophy, and get him back to the Royal Hotel in time for a late lunch and an evening of pub-hopping and native entertainment.

I stuck around a few months, hoping I might find something that would convince me I was wrong. Even had a couple of jobs offered to me as a park warden. I almost took one; I got as far as negotiating the right to do some limited hunting, just for my dinner pot, but in the end I turned it down. Nothing wrong with the kind of people who come out to the parks, but they weren't *my* kind of people. I could understand camera buffs like Walker, who I'd taken out four or five times; he'd stand there taking holos of a charging Demoncat and get furious with me if I tried to turn it before it got within ten yards of him, or he'd climb into a tree to get a holo of a Bush Devil eating a Silvercoat it had dragged up there to keep it safe from scavengers. But I had no interest in the kind of camera hunters who would drive across the parks, intent only on the number of animals they could holo in a day's time, and I had a feeling they would outnumber the Walkers by hundreds to one.

Then there was the matter of poaching. A number of wags had set up shops in Berengi and the other towns, and there was no question that their tribal brothers were supplying them with illegal eyestones. In fact, it was the Dorado and the Kia who brought the Sabrehorn to extinction, not Men. And there was no way you were going to close down a poaching operation if the wags wouldn't testify against their tribal brothers. So I just couldn't see any future in the game warden business.

I considered buying a farm in the Greenlands up beyond Berengi, but I was used to walking across the land, not digging in it. I even looked into taking on some younger partners in my safari company and spending most of my time in Berengi, but Berengi was just a town, and I didn't like towns. Besides, I had all the money I needed, and I didn't propose to spend the rest of my life working at a job that I didn't like.

In the end, I suppose I was just wasting a little time, trying to get all the images of Peponi set in my mind, before I left it for good. And there was never any question about coming back: no one ever goes back to Peponi. Whatever it was that brought you there has got to change before you leave, and once it *has* changed, you don't want to see what it's become. It wasn't just the hunters who felt that way; even Amanda Pickett hasn't been back there since Buko Pepon took over—and he tried like hell to get her back. Even named a district after her, and they've never done that for any other human.

I suppose I ought to make it clear: it wasn't Peponi that was dying. It was growing by leaps and bounds, and a steady stream of Men kept immigrating there. What was dying was a way of life that had existed on Peponi. I suppose that the old-timers, the men like Fuentes and Bocci and Hakira and Hellfire Bailey and Catamount Greene and me, were very much like the Landships and the Sabrehorns and the Demoncats: we were colorful and we created a lot of interest in the world, but now that civilization was spreading across the face of the planet, we simply weren't necessary anymore. You could never tell when one of us, an old hunter or an old Demoncat, might frighten an investor off. And since we were as wild as the animals, they never could quite trust us to behave the way we were supposed to. We were a potential embarrassment at best, a potential source of disaster at worst; they weren't exactly sorry to have had us, but they sure weren't sorry to lose us either.

People still go to Peponi to see its beauties and its animals, and they still enjoy themselves; they visit the cities and the game parks, they ski down the mountains and swim in the oceans, they visit the wags in their villages and their cities, and they go home with wonderful stories to tell.

But they'll never set off on a trip down a river, or through the high savannah, and know that they were the first to ever see this particular place. They'll never know the feeling you get when you see a herd of Silvercoats so big that it takes them a full day to pass by. They'll never see a Landship or a Sabrehorn, except in a museum. They won't wake up in the morning, hundreds of miles from the nearest town, with the knowledge that they're free to go anywhere and do anything they please, that a whole world is there for the taking. They'll smell the air and see the flowers and watch the avians circling overhead, and if they're lucky they might see a carnivore on a kill, but it won't be the same. For one thing, they'll be on a schedule—here in the morning, there at noon, someplace else at dusk—while there were times, back in the old days, when I couldn't even have told you what month it was. If they're late getting back to Berengi, they'll miss their flight connections and panic their travel agents; if I was two or three weeks or months late returning to Berengi after a hunt, anyone who was waiting for me would still be there, drinking in the Thunderhead Bar, or they would have left a note for me on the Message Tree in front of the Equator Hotel. The Peponi I knew didn't have any calenders or clocks or fences, and that Peponi is gone forever.

I arrived on Peponi a few years too late, but I left at the right time. Whatever it's become now, I don't want to know about it.

I brought nothing with me to Peponi; I took nothing out.

I have no regrets.

DIGGING THE TOMBS

Another trip to Africa, another diary
for Lan's Lantern. *It has become almost*
automatic now.

1988: Things got out of hand early. Carol and I had decided to take a trip to Egypt, and add a week in Tanzania at the end of it. When Pat and Roger Sims heard about it, they decided that they would like to come along. So did my agent, Eleanor Wood. So did her two kids. So did my father and two of his friends.

Readers of these diaries will know that Carol and I always go to Africa with a private guide. But with a party of 10, this was out of the question...so we started doing a little homework. We knew we wanted to stay at the Ramses Hilton, as it gets a 5-star rating from the Egyptian government and is the only Cairo hotel which had never had a reported case of dysentary or botulism. We also wanted to cruise the Nile on either the *Osiris* or the *Isis*, the two top-rated cruise ships. As for tour companies, there were two that stood out: R & H Voyages in Egypt and Ranger Safaris in Tanzania. And, since Carol and I know Nairobi inside out, we didn't want to pay a penny for laying over there for a couple of days; we had friends there to drive us around, and a tour guide would be an unnecessary expense.

So I called Gametrackers, one of the better packagers of African trips, and told them what I wanted. They could do some of it, they said, but not all.

Too bad, I said; you just lost a party of ten. Wait, they said; we'll look into it further. You do that, I said. Well, maybe we can get Ranger, they said a few hours later, but R & H is out of the question. Nice knowing you, I said. Well, perhaps we can get R & H, they said two days later, but we'll have to charge you for the Kenya portion. Not a chance, I said. Hold on, they said; do you really have a guaranteed party of ten?

And, 27 long-distance phone calls and five weeks later, we finally had exactly the itinerary and the tour guides that we wanted.

February 8, 1989: We flew to England via Detroit, so that we could pick up Pat and Roger along the way. What we didn't know was that the plane stopped to refuel in Toronto, where it also picked up most of its passengers.

Why did that make a difference?

Because we were all dressed for summer, and once we stopped in Toronto it was announced that passengers going through to England were not allowed a) to leave the plane, or b) use the bathrooms. Then they opened all the doors to load food, water, and whatever—and in came a howling, five-below-zero wind, and we were forbidden even to lock ourselves in the bathrooms to hide from it. They left the doors open for 45 minutes, at the end of which we resembled four slightly blue popsicles.

I just love British Airways.

February 9: We joined up with the rest of our party at the Heathrow Airport in London, and Eleanor immediately gave me the galleys to *Paradise,* which Tor had thoughtfully arranged for me to proofread while everyone else was enjoying the Nile cruise, and off we went to Cairo.

The Hilton was large and impressive and luxurious, and while the rest of us slept the sleep of the innocent, Eleanor spent most of the night at the local hospital, watching them stitch up her son's head after he split it open falling down some stairs.

Not the most auspicious beginning.

February 10: I had met with our Cairo guide, an Egyptologist named Iman, who loves Americans and hates Khadaffi, the previous night, and told him that we wanted a hell of a lot more than the usual 45 minutes at the Egyptian Museum, so he picked us up right after breakfast and took us there for the entire morning, which was about ten days short of being sufficient time to see it all. The museum holds scores of mummies, the entire contents of Tut's tomb, the first painting ever created, and about half a million other fascinating items. There is simply no way to begin doing it justice in less than a week, and when next we go to Egypt, we have every intention of spending a full week there. Then it was off to Islamic Cairo, which reminded me a lot of the seedier portions of Mombasa, and to Coptic Cairo, where we saw the first Christian church in Egypt, the first mosque, and the Ben Ezra Temple (where, theoretically, Jesus, Mary and Joseph were hidden during part of their [theoretical] stay in Egypt). We also visited the Papyrus Institute, where we picked up some authentic papyrus artwork (as opposed to the phony stuff they sell on every street corner), and then it was off to a lovely outdoor restaurant, well off the tourist trail, for lunch, where Iman, who had been giving us a condensed college course in Egyptian history, finally paused for breath.

In the afternoon we went to the pyramids at Giza. Everyone has seen pictures of them, of course, but photos lack a certain scale, which was best supplied by Napoleon's scientists, who calculated that if the pyramid of Cheops were disassembled, they could use it to build a wall one meter high and 30 inches wide around the entirety of France: it consists of 2,300,000 blocks each weighing from 2 to 15 tons. Being an assiduous student of terrible Hollywood epics, I had assumed that the pyramids had been built by slave labor, but Iman explained that while slaves supplied food and water to the workers, they were in fact built by volunteer Egyptian labor, who felt that they were destined to go to Heaven by virtue of having worked on such holy structures. Each pyramid took about 20 years to build, and they only worked on them three months a year, during the rainy season, when they were able to leave their farms.

We then went to the Perfume Institute, where they press the flowers and create the scents which are then shipped off to Paris, where alcohol, designer labels, and huge pricetags are added. Carol, for example, spends about $60.00 for a quarter-ounce of Opium, her regular perfume. We bought an entire ounce of its essence for $10.00, took it home with us, and will now add nine ounces of pure alcohol; if it works, we'll have $2,400.00 worth of Opium for a total outlay of about $15.00. (And if not, just anticipating the savings has already given us $15.00 worth of guilty pleasure.)

After dark, we went back to the pyramids and the sphinx for the light show, which runs in a different language every hour. Very impressive—and, given the time of year, *very* chilly.

February 11: The day began with a delightful drive out to Memphis, where we saw no end of enormous statues that had been buried and forgotten for, literally, millennia. We then stopped by a rug-weaving factory, which employs only pre-pubescent boys on the assumption that only their fingers are small and limber enough for the work required. (Everybody involved in the project spent an inordinate length of time explaining to us that this was actually a school, the children were exceptionally well-paid, and this therefore didn't really constitute child labor. When all was said and done, however, there was a lot of labor going on, and all of it was being done by children.)

Next we visited the 6,000-year-old "Step Pyramid" at Saqqara, the very first pyramid ever built. (Architect #1: "Hey, Harry, wait'll you see the plans for this joker's tomb." Architect #2: "Not very cost-effective. It'll never catch on." But it *did* catch on: 69 Egyptian pyramids have been discovered thus far, though a number of them were created out of limestone and have lost their structural integrity.)

Iman took us to another off-the-beaten-path outdoor restaurant for lunch. This one had about twenty feral dogs living on the grounds, and they had grown so fat off table scraps and garbage pits that they actually turned their noses up when we offered them anything but meat. (In fact, Cairo and the surrounding area are absolutely filled with feral dogs—some of them, thanks to a regular supply of tourist handouts, considerably less feral than others.)

After we had finished feeding ourselves and the dogs, we drove to the Citadel, which was built to defend Cairo against Richard the Lion Hearted and his Crusaders, and is distinguished by the Mosque of Mohammed Ali (the Turk, not the boxer). When night fell we returned to the hotel, freshened up, and went out to a nightclub that featured some top-notch belly dancers and a young man who did what I can only call a Whirling Dervish dance, in which he spun around in circles, non-stop, for the better part of fifteen minutes; makes me dizzy just to remember it.

February 12: We left Cairo and flew to Luxor, a very pleasant change since Cairo has a population of 15 million, polution you wouldn't believe, and traffic that resembles Manhattan at rush hour. Luxor is a much smaller, more tranquil city, and we immediately transferred to the *Osiris*, a Hilton-owned ship which has a couple of restaurants, three bars, and a swimming pool.

And it was there that we met M. Hamdy M. Ismael, who was to change our lives for the next five days. Hamdy holds a Ph.D. in Egyptology and speaks three languages fluently, but he makes far more money from tips as one of the two resident guides of the *Osiris* than he could possibly make teaching in the university. More to the point, he has the soul of a track coach and the heart of a drill sergeant. It was Hamdy's job to teach the English speakers aboard the ship (we were outnumbered about 2-to-1 by the French) absolutely everything he knew about his country, and with only five days in which to do it, he knew he had no time to waste. He also believed in the show-and-tell principle; he would never describe any monument that he could make us run to, and he would never recite any hieroglyph or cartouche that he could make us climb and see for ourselves. He was also a strong believer in visual aids; no day began without a variety of photos, maps, diagrams and posters of what we were to see.

After we unpacked and had lunch, Hamdy took us to the temple at Karnak, which I think is the single most impressive structure I saw in Egypt. It was begun in the 12th Dynasty and completed in the 20th, and could easily hold a trio of football fields in its 22-acre interior. There are 134 columns, each 10 feet in diameter and about 60 feet high, there are a pair of 143-foot-high obelisks, there are about a zillion stone rams which once formed an avenue reaching all the way to the temple at Luxor, there are numerous enormous statues of Ramses II, and finally, there is a sacred lake. There are also chairs and refreshments, but Hamdy made sure we never saw them, since it would have cut into his lecture time.

(By the way, for those of you who may have seen documentaries on Egypt's various temples, you will doubtless have noticed that they are a] always crowded with tourists, and that b] the tourists always cluster together in groups of from ten to thirty. This is because each group follows a guide who speaks their language. There are always English, French, German, Egyptian, and Japanese-speaking groups, and on any given day you can find five or six other languages being bandied about.)

After three hours at Karnak—and it took three hours just to walk from one end to the other and see it all—we drove a few miles away to the temple at Luxor, which would have been damned impressive had we not seen Karnak first. Then Hamdy went off to run laps around the upper deck and left us to eat dinner in peace. We later returned to Karnak for the most impressive sound and light show of the trip, and collapsed in our bunks at about nine o'clock, as Hamdy had warned us that after such an easy day, we had a lot of ground to make up in the morning.

February 13: Hamdy woke us up so early that we could still see our breath (a rarity in Egypt, unless you happen to be getting a complete 4-year Egyptology course crammed into 120 hours), and took us off to the temple at Dendara. We then rode through some beautiful Egyptian countryside (beautiful as long as we stayed within sight of the Nile, that is; it was desert anywhere more than half a mile from the river) to the temple of Seti I at Abydos, and finally to the tomb of Osiris. Hamdy then very reluctantly and begrudgingly told us that we had the afternoon to ourselves—it took all his will power not to give us a written exam on what we had already seen—and while everyone else sat on deck and sipped cool drinks and watched the Nile go by, yours truly got to spend the next six hours proofreading his goddamned galleys for his exceptionally thoughtful publisher, who had promised to deliver them no later than January 5.

I assume we passed several fascinating and beautiful sights, but deep in my heart I hope we didn't.

February 14: This was Valley of the Kings day, and even without Hamdy's warning, we knew that we were going to do a lot of walking.

We drove past the Colossi of Memnon, which in truth were rather dismal failures in their job of spiritual scarecrows, since of all the tombs only Tut's was unplundered, and began with the Valley of the Queens, which covers a couple of hundred acres and houses perhaps 50 tombs.

That was just a warm-up. Then we visited the funerary temple of Hatchepsut, the only female pharaoh. (Easy name to remember: hat + cheap suit.)

Finally we got to the Valley of the Kings, where they have discovered 62 tombs, the most recent being Tut's in 1922, and where they think there may be six or seven more as yet undiscovered, but they haven't been able to get the funding to finance a thorough search.

Tut's tomb itself is amazingly unimpressive, four little rooms about the size of a small apartment. When you realize that they filled half of the second floor of the Egyptian Museum with the artifacts they found here, you have to wonder what some of the other tombs contained before they were plundered by grave robbers. The tomb of Ramses III, for instance, goes on for almost half a mile, and has large chambers every few feet; one could probably have filled the entire Smithsonian with what was carried away from there.

After we had seen three or four tombs, Hamdy gave us half an hour to explore any tombs we wished. 90% of our group decided to explore the bar and restaurant instead. Carol and Roger tried the tomb of Amenophis III, which was reached by climbing about three stories straight up and then entering a tiny hole and climbing three stories straight down. It looked too strenuous to me, so I chose the tomb of a lesser pharaoh, which had a nice simple stairway. When I had gone down 300 stairs, I finally came to someone struggling up the staircase, which at least assured me that I wasn't decending to Hades. I kept going, past granite walls with no artwork or hieroglyphs at all until, 573 stairs later, I reached the burial chamber...and came to an empty crypt and a single painting, somewhat faded. I was somewhat faded myself, between the exertion and the lack of air, so I immediately turned around and spent the next 15 minutes climbing back up to ground level. I had just dragged myself to the bar and ordered a beer when Hamdy, bouncing on his toes like Mike Tyson warming up for the opening bell, stopped by to tell me the bus was leaving. Our next stop was the Ramasseum, another funerary temple, this one for Ramses III (who, despite the temple and the tomb, doesn't hold a candle to Ramses II as an egomaniac), and then we returned to the boat for lunch. I don't know what anyone else did in the afternoon, but I stayed aboard and finished proofing my galleys, courtesy of the thoughtful people at Tor. A couple of Americans stopped to look over my shoulder, realized I was a science fiction writer, and spent the next couple of hours asking if Isaac Asimov really wrote all those books himself and why don't they write really mature sci-fi like *Star Trek* anymore?

February 15: The boat docked at Esna, and we transferred to horse-drawn carriages to get to the Esna temple. The horses were the first unhealthy animals I had seen in Egypt—all the stray dogs and cats were incredibly fat—and since our guides had handled all the *baksheesh* up to this point, it was just a bit disconcerting to find, once we had paid for the carriage ride, that the horse needed a pound, his bridle needed 50 piasters, and his shoes needed another 10 piasters. We paid rather than argued, since it came to all of about 50 cents.

(I might point out here that all bargaining at the ever-present bazaars—which have sprung up around every tourist attraction—is a two-fold negotiation: first you reach a price, and then you have to do it all over again when they tell you with wide innocent eyes that they thought you meant English rather than Egyptian pounds, a difference of merely 500%.)

We returned to the boat for lunch, where Roger became the first of our party to get sick on foreign food and spent the rest of the day in bed, and then, just because the horses needed a workout, we took carriages again, this time to the temple of Edfu, where I finally got an idea for a novel. It'll be a horror story, and I'm collaborating on it with George Alec Effinger, who, after producing *When Gravity Fails* and *A Fire in the Sun*, certainly has the background in Islam to make it work.

February 16: We docked at Kom-Ombo and walked up the gangplank right to the temple, which would have been a lot more impressive had I not been all templed out at this point.

The boat then went on to Aswan, where we took a felluca ride (rather like a sturdy dhow or a cheap sailboat) to Elephantine Island to see the lovely and extensive botannical gardens and the tomb of the Aga Khan (and where my father joined Roger in the sick bay).

We bid Hamdy an exhausted (but well-educated) good-bye and drove out to the airport to catch a plane to Abu Simbel. The plane had already taken off, but R & H isn't ranked #1 among Egyptian tour companies for nothing, and they actually had the clout to call it back and get it to land again to pick us up, much to the disgust of the passengers who were already on board.

Abu Simbel is, after Karnak, the most impressive sight in Egypt, a temple carved out of a mountain—and is even more impressive when you realize that they had to raise the entire structure forty-three feet to avoid it being flooded when they built the High Dam at Aswan. The colors of the paintings on the interior of the temple are exquisite, having withstood the eons much better than those we had seen everywhere else except perhaps in Tut's tomb.

As night fell we flew back to Cairo, where Eleanor and her children departed from our group—she had elected not to go on to Tanzania, and besides, *some*one had to deliver the goddamned galleys to Tor—and the rest of us caught a midnight plane to Kenya. It was the much-feared and much-maligned Egyptair flight, which, surprisingly, was the only flight we took the whole trip that departed and arrived on time.

February 17: We landed in Nairobi at 6:30 in the morning, and suddenly I felt energized, as I always do in Kenya. It was like being home again.

Our friend Perry Mason picked us up at the airport—after getting *Ivory* dedicated to him, and having two different characters based on him in *Paradise*, it was the very least he could do—and took us to the Norfolk Hotel, which remains the best place to stay in Nairobi. While everyone else slept and/or unpacked, I hung around the lobby, and spent some time visiting with Perry's departing safari clients. (He's got Arlene Dahl and Jane Powell coming in next.)

In the early afternoon I took Pat and Roger to the Nairobi Museum, and then led them around the city center, pointing out various sights and landmarks to them. When we stopped in at the East African Wildlife Society, I found, to my surprise, that I'm getting to be a very well-known writer in Kenya, thanks to Perry twisting every arm he can grab and forcing my books on them, and to the Wildlife Society's gift shop selling copies of all my African science fiction.

Everyone but me was pretty tired from the trip, so instead of the usual dinner at the Carnivore or the Horseman, we all ate at the hotel and turned in early. (Except for me: I spent a few hours speaking to various members of the Kikuyu staff, looking for material for more "Kirinyaga" stories. Found some, too.)

February 18: While my father and his friends slept in and had a late breakfast, I arranged for Perry to give us and Pat and Roger a game run through the Nairobi National Park. They were considering coming on safari in Kenya with us in 1991, and it seemed like an excellent opportunity for them to get to know Perry and compare his services with those we'd be receiving in

Tanzania. (It worked; God and finances willing, they're coming back with us in 1991. Carol and I will also be spending a month in Botswana and Zimbabwe in 1990, and will possibly be able to add a week in Malawi as well.)

We also had Perry stop by the animal orphanage, which is run by Daphne Sheldrick, who wrote *The Orphans of Tsavo* (and starred in the television documentary of the same name), then left him to catch up on his paperwork, grabbed a quick lunch at the Norfolk, and then went shopping at the Inter-Continental Hotel (which has the best gift shops in Nairobi).

Finally we met Perry for dinner at Marino's, an Italian restaurant which is owned by a business associate of his, and had an excellent meal. (In fact, once you know your way around, it's almost impossible *not* to eat like a king in Kenya.)

By the time we got back to the Norfolk, someone on the hotel's staff had placed my name with my books, and nothing would do but that I pose for some photographs for their monthly newsletter. I hope they remember to send me one.

February 19: We were picked up by a local safari company at 7:00 in the morning, driven to the Tanzania border, and transferred into the keeping of Ranger Safaris once we cleared customs. Our driver, the one who would be with us for the next five days, was a Chagga named Muro, who had grown up on the slopes of nearby Mount Kilimanjaro. He hadn't read *Ivory*, but we got to discussing the Kilimanjaro Elephant (whose tusks form the subject matter of the book), and he feels that, based on my information, he probably walked over the spot where the elephant died many times in his youth.

Arusha isn't much of a town, but we needed lunch, so we stopped there for a surprisingly elegant buffet at the Mount Meru Hotel, and then continued on to the Ngorongoro Crater, which I had been longing to see since I first read about it at the age of ten, in 1952. Once we were about 30 miles south of Arusha the roads became as bad as any I'd ever seen, and how we managed to average 40 miles an hour on them without blowing all four tires and breaking both axles will forever remain a mystery to me.

The Crater was everything I had hoped it would be, though we arrived too late to descend into it that day, and spent the night in the Ngorongoro Crater Lodge. They had a telescope on one of the decks, and I was able to spot about half a dozen elephants and a cheetah for our party. (It's just a matter of knowing their habits and figuring out where to look for them at a particular time of day. Carol, who knows this as well as I do, was umimpressed; I graciously allowed the rest of them to think of me as Stewart Granger with a receding hairline.)

February 20: If you had but a single day to see a microcosm of African wildlife, if you could only take one game run in your life, you would be well-advised to spend that day and take that game run in the Ngorongoro Crater.

The Crater itself is a caldera, or collapsed volcano. In fact, before it collapsed, it was a considerably bigger mountain than Kilimanjaro, which is currently the largest mountain in Africa. The floor of the Crater is about 2,500 feet below the rim, some ten miles in diameter, and is mostly a grassy plain, though heavily dotted with lakes and forests. Every East African animal exists within its confines, with two exceptions: there are no impalas (they don't find the vegetation to their taste) and no giraffes (they couldn't climb down the slopes).

The drive down from the rim takes almost an hour, and can be accomplished only with a four-wheel drive vehicle. Once within the Crater, it's almost impossible *not* to run into enormous herds of game wherever you go. Within ten minutes we had passed hundreds of hartebeest and thousands of zebra and wildebeest, and were parked about fifteen feet away from the patriarch of the Crater's elephants, a magnificent creature carrying almost eighty pounds of ivory on each side. (In fact, I saw a dozen elephants carrying better than 50 pounds a side, which is twelve more than I've seen during almost two months in Kenya.)

The rarest of the big mammals in Africa, and the one in the most immediate danger of extinction, is the black rhino. We saw seven of them within our first two hours in the Crater. In fact, one of them even charged our Land Rover, stopping about five feet from my door. (I ducked, but I kept my video camera running, and got the entire episode on tape.)

There were lions galore, and huge herds of buffalo, and birdlife that birdwatchers like Carol only dream about. (More than 450 species of birds have been observed in the Crater; we must have seen close to 300 before we left.) We came across the body of a freshly-poached elephant who had died the night before—not even the Crater is safe from poachers—and got tape of about a hundred vultures dining on his enormous carcass. We had lunch by a delightful hippo pool, where Roger didn't protect his lunch very well and lost it to some dive-bombing kites. We saw a wildebeest foal being born. And finally we returned to the rim of the Crater for dinner, totally overwhelmed by the most productive game run we had ever taken. Pat and Roger, who had been only to the Nairobi Park, and my father's friends, who had never been on a game run before, did not realize then—and may not even realize now—just what a fabulous paradise the Ngorongoro Crater is...but after driving through the world-famous Serengeti Plains the next two days and seeing nothing to equal this, they may have some inkling that the Crater is Special with a capital "S".

February 21: We left the Crater at daybreak and set off for the Serengeti. Most travelers stay in the Seronara Lodge (which is frequently out of food, water and power), because it's nearer the flat grasslands that attract the great herds, but I had always wanted to see Lobo Lodge, which is much farther north but had won a number of architectural awards when it was built in 1973 (and which has never been out of water or power.)

It was an all-day ride, but it was actually an all-day game run as well. We stopped at the Olduvai Gorge for about half an hour, which is really all it's worth. The Leakeys built a tiny museum there, no more than thirty feet on a side, and the gorge itself looks like any other gorge unless you're an anthropologist who knows what he's looking for.

By ten in the morning we had entered Serengeti, probably the world's most famous game park, and at 5900 square miles one of the larger ones. The migrating wildebeest herds were at the south end, and we saw bits and pieces of them as we drove off the main track in search of cheetahs and lions, both of which we found. We hit Seronara at noontime, stopped for lunch, and then went north for a few hours to Lobo, taking detours to spot game all along the way. The Lobo Lodge is everything it was cracked up to be. It's built amidst huge granite boulders, and the boulders frequently form the walls of the multi-leveled lodge. In fact, there's a swimming pool that has been carved entirely out of a granite rock. The entire lodge overlooks the Serengeti plains, and there's a water hole right below it, so one can observe the animals drinking at dawn and sunset. While Lobo doesn't measure up to some of Kenya's lodges in luxury—it's a far cry from the Mount Kenya Safari Club or the Samburu Lodge, for example—it is nonetheless the most beautiful single structure we've stayed at during all our African travels.

The baboons think so too. They spent most of the night running over the roof and trying to get into our rooms through the windows.

February 22: We took a pair of game runs, but due to the unseasonal rain (which meant water was available just about everywhere), the animals were pretty well-dispersed, and we settled for hunting up some of the rarer birds and mammals. At one point we went off the road in a likely-looking direction, and drove for almost an hour without seeing a living thing. Just as I was about to explain the old colonial acronym *Mamoba* ("Mile after mile of bloody Africa") we ran into a herd of buffalo, and things picked up from there.

February 23: We left Lobo before sunrise, drove south through the Serengeti, and reached the Lake Manyara National Park in time for lunch.

It was rather sad. Lake Manyara, a tiny park by African standards, used to have the highest concentration of elephants in the world. Perry told us that a decade ago it wasn't unusual to see 300 in a day.

All that has changed. The elephants are pretty much poached out, the rhinos are totally poached out, and the poachers have now begun concentrating on anything they can eat, which means that except for the ever-present baboons, just about every animal (and there aren't that many of them left) races away hell for leather as soon as a human or a vehicle gets within 150 yards of it. We did get some footage of hippos fighting in a pool, but by and large what we saw was a very lovely, very empty park that the government hasn't had the funds or the manpower to protect.

February 24: We left in the morning, explained rather forcefully to Muro (who obviously had orders to take us there) that we had no intention of shopping in Arusha, and instead stopped for lunch at a brand-new lodge Ranger Safaris has constructed in the midst of a coffee plantation on a private, spring-fed lake about 15 miles out of Arusha. It's quite lovely, and not only has the standard restaurant and bar, but a tandouri as well. It had only been open about three weeks, but it was already doing quite a bit of business.

Then it was back to Nairobi. When we arrived at
the Norfolk we were too late to get our reserved rooms,
so they gave us cottages instead. (In the old days—and
the Norfolk has been around since 1906—most of their
guests were on hunting safaris, which frequently took
from three to six months. The guests would stay in
Nairobi while rounding up their help and outfitting
themselves; they frequently possessed a dozen or more
trunks, and a room simply couldn't accomodate them, so
the hotel built a number of elegant two-and-three-room
cottages. One of the men at the desk told me that Carol
and I had been given the cottage where Robert Ruark
lived for five months while he was writing *Uhuru*.) The
Norfolk's Ibis Grill is probably the finest restaurant in
Nairobi, but it seemed a shame not to use the cottage, so
we picked up the Ibis' menu and ordered from it through
room service. It was so enjoyable that we have decided
that from now on, no matter what the cost, when we're
in Nairobi we not only stay at the Norfolk, but in the
Norfolk's cottages. (Ours and Ruark's was #5; I gather
Hemingway was partial to #7.)

February 25: I forgot to warn our party about the
extortion that goes on at Third World airports, and
Roger and my father's friends both wound up paying a
few extra dollars to make sure their bags got on the
plane to London. We took off on schedule, but a few
hours into the trip our pilot announced that we had
been fighting a 180-mile-per-hour headwind for quite
some time, and that we no longer had enough fuel to
reach London, not the most encouraging message one
might wish for six hours into the flight. So we set down
in Rome to refuel, arrived in London four hours later
(good old trustworthy British Airways again), and
checked into the Heathrow Holiday Inn with Pat and
Roger, while my father and his friends went their own
way.
Our room was #207, and when we got there, we
found that someone had neglected to give it a closet. So

I went down to the desk and asked for a new room. They gave me #212, which was perfectly acceptable until 3:00 AM when suddenly the radio began blaring at full volume. It was the Tyson-Bruno fight, and I told Carol I'd fix it as soon as Tyson put Bruno away, which didn't figure to take more than a couple of minutes.

When the fight had concluded, I began fiddling with the knobs and dials, but I couldn't turn the damned thing off, so I called down to the desk for help. They sent someone up a moment later. He couldn't turn it off either. Then, about five minutes into his labors, he frowned, placed his ear against the wall, and announced that it wasn't *our* radio at all, but the one next door. He called the guy in #210 and asked him to tone it down, which worked until eight in the morning, when our thoughtful neighbor began playing acid rock at full volume. You not only could hear it from our room; you could hear it from the elevator half a building away.

February 26: We gave our neighbor until noon to get his fill of 500-decibel rock music, then went to the desk and asked for a new room. They gave us #262, in a different wing of the hotel, and we spend the rest of the afternoon loafing around the hotel and its pool. We went into London to have dinner at the Bombay Brasserie (which is a beautiful restaurant, properly done up in colonial style, but the food isn't as good as that of its main rival, The Last Days of the Raj).

Upon returning, we opened the door to our room and found that it had been ransacked by a thief. We immediately called the hotel's security chief, and began trying to find out what was missing. It was almost unbelievable: with $5,000 of camera gear and triple that in jewelry to choose from, our thief stole just three things--a pair of broken binoculars, a pair of sunglasses, and a copy of Egan Romney's *Guide to London Restaurants*. I suspect he's not long for this line of work.

So, at two in the morning, we moved into #301--I know it's a lot of room numbers to remember, but bear with me--our fourth room in 32 hours.

And people think Africa is exciting.

February 27: Everyone else went shopping, while I stopped by Century/Hutchison Books and let Deborah Beale, my British editor, take me out to lunch. I did enough business with her to pay for my next safari, so I celebrated by picking up some rare Africana for my library at Rowland Ward's British branch. We spent the evening in the theater watching a 4-million-pound bomb, a musical based on Fritz Lang's *Metropolis*. I think the entire budget was spent on the magnificent sets; they'd have done better if they'd have spent a couple of hundred dollars on a script and score. We walked out in the middle of the second act; Pat and Roger waited until the audience began roaring with laughter during Brian Blessed's most tragic moment, then joined us.

February 28: When I went to check out, the computer decided that I had simultaneously been occupying #207, #212, #262 and #301 for three days, and tried to bill me for all four rooms. (See? I told you to bear with me.) It took half an hour to sort things out. I just love computers.

The plane to the States was only a couple of hours late (British Airways again, natch), and we got home to a six-foot stack of mail. The very first thing I opened was a letter telling me that "Kirinyaga" had made the Nebula Ballot. It made me almost glad to be home again.

Sigh. Only 463 days to Zimbabwe and Botswana.